BRIDGES

Christians Connecting with Muslims

Companion Study Book

crescent project
HOPE WORTH SHARING

"Crescent Project's *Bridges* study is an excellent resource for small groups. It cultivates a heart for others and develops a missional focus in a natural and simple way. I highly recommend it as a small group study"
— Jon Weiner,
   Southeast Christian Church

"I deeply appreciate Crescent Project's compelling blend of truth and love in dealing with our Muslim friends. They beautifully balance the two parts of 1 Peter 3:15: 'Make a defense,' but do so 'with gentleness and respect.' I cheer them on and recommend their message to anyone interested in reaching out to the Muslims around us."
— Mark Mittelberg, author of *Choosing Your Faith* and coauthor of *The Unexpected Adventure*

© 2014 Fouad Masri
Fourth printing 2014

No part of this book may be reproduced or transmitted in any form or by any means, electronic or mechanical, including photocopying and recording or by any information storage or retrieval system, except as may be expressly permitted in writing by the publisher. Requests for permission should be addressed in writing to Fouad Masri; P.O. Box 50986, Indianapolis, IN 46250 USA.

ISBN 978-1-4158-6902-4

All Scripture quotations are taken from the Holman Christian Standard Bible®, copyright © 1999, 2000, 2002, 2003, 2009 by Holman Bible Publishers. Used by permission. *Bridges: Christians Connecting with Muslims* is a trademark of Crescent Project. Quotations from the Qur'an are from The Qur'an Translation, 7th edition, by Abdullah Yusef Ali (Elmhurst, NY: Tahrike Tarsile Quran Inc., 2001). Design: Alesa Bahler, Legacy Design

To order additional copies of this resource, write to Crescent Project; P.O. Box 50986, Indianapolis, IN 46250 USA; e-mail info@crescentproject.org; phone toll free (800) 446-5457

Order online at:
www.crescentproject.org
www.fouadmasri.com.

Printed in the United States of America

Crescent Project
P.O. Box 50986
Indianapolis, IN 46150

 Dear *Bridges* Participant,

Do Muslims seem mysterious or unknowable to you? The images on TV of hostile Muslims can strike fear in us; pictures of veiled women can cause us to think Muslims are unapproachable, not to mention unreachable!

I'm so glad you are overcoming fear and taking a step toward understanding Muslims. Seven million Muslims live and work among us in North America, and each one needs—*and deserves*—an authentic Christian witness. My prayer is that you will grow in compassion and understanding for Muslims and will be moved to share the hope of Christ with a Muslim.

Bridges includes six sessions made up of prayer, discussion, video content, group response, and action assignments. All of these components are meant to develop a better understanding of Islam and to give you the heart of an ambassador as you relate to Muslims.

- ✣ The group discussions give you an opportunity to share your ideas, ask questions, and help one another understand and learn the material.
- ✣ The video sessions include testimonies, interviews, and the major instructional content. Don't omit them!
- ✣ The action assignments are practical responses to the material, completed outside the session. They require an investment of time, preparation, and prayer.

"Christ's love compels us, since we have reached this conclusion: If One died for all, then all died" (2 Corinthians 5:14).

Over the next six sessions don't lose sight of the goal: Muslims need and deserve an authentic Christian witness. And remember the motivation behind it all: the love of Christ compels us to share His good news with Muslims.

Reaching Muslims for Christ,

Fouad Masri

Fouad Masri
President and Founder
Crescent Project

www.fouadmasri.com
www.crescentproject.org
www.crescentproject.tv

TABLE OF CONTENTS

Session 1: Islam Rising 7

Session 2: Belief and Ritual 19

Session 3: Attitudes of an Ambassador 33

Session 4: Bridging the Gospel 45

Session 5: Understanding the New Testament's Credibility . . . 55

Session 6: Understanding Jesus' Sacrifice 69

Leader's Notes 85

Bonus Book: Is the Injeel Corrupted? 101

Bonus Book: Adha in the Injeel 133

Bridges: Christians Connecting with Muslims

Crescent Project

www.crescentproject.org

Crescent Project is a valuable resource for reaching out to your Muslim friends.

Additional resources are available at the author's website: www.fouadmasri.com

crescent project
HOPE WORTH SHARING

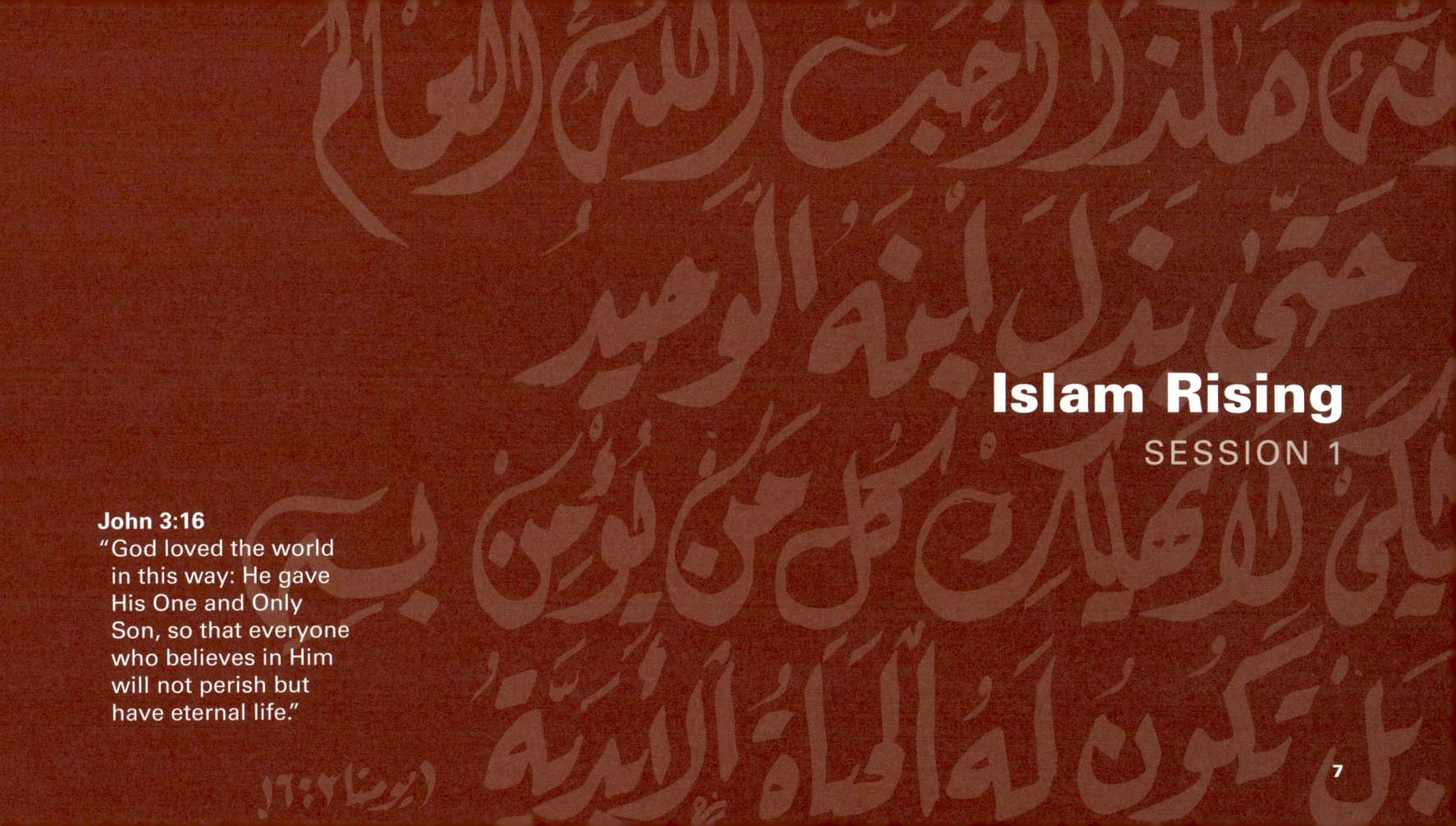

Matthew 7:7
"Keep asking, and it will be given to you. Keep searching, and you will find. Keep knocking, and the door will be opened to you."

SESSION 1
ISLAM RISING

AFTER THIS SESSION YOU WILL UNDERSTAND:

✢ Islam's beginning.

✢ How the religion spread.

✢ Who Muhammad was and how he lived his life.

✢ The difference between the Qur'an and the Hadith.

PRAY GOD WILL CULTIVATE IN YOU:

✢ A heart to care about Muslims.

✢ Eyes to see them.

✢ Actions to follow learning.

Bridges: Christians Connecting with Muslims

WARM-UP

In the spaces below, write two things you already know about Islam and two things you'd like to learn.

WHAT I ALREADY KNOW ABOUT ISLAM

1.

2.

WHAT I WOULD LIKE TO LEARN ABOUT ISLAM AND MUSLIMS

1.

2.

Watch video session 1 and fill in the corresponding blanks.

Downloads of this book and video session can be purchased at *www.crescentproject.org* or *www.fouadmasri.com*.

VIDEO SESSION 1
ISLAM RISING

FOUNDING OF ISLAM

MUHAMMAD, THE MAN

Muhammad was born in _____ into the Quraysh tribe (highest tribe in Mecca). His mother died when he was 6 years old, and he was raised by his uncle, Abu Talib.

Arabian society before Islam:
- Pagan _____ society with more than 360 gods in the Ka'aba
- Arabs from the line of Ishmael originally worshiped one God
- Warring tribes
- Traveling caravans brought contact with Jews and Christians.

A.D. 595: At age 25 Muhammad married his employer, a wealthy widow named Khadijah. She provided him social and financial security.

Acts 2:4-11
"... both Jews and proselytes, Cretans and Arabs—we hear them speaking the magnificent acts of God in our own languages."

Life of Muhammad	A.D. 570	A.D. 595	A.D. 610
	He was born in Mecca.	He married a 40-year-old wealthy widow, Khadijah.	He had his first revelation.

Islam Rising

A.D. 622	A.D. 622	A.D. 630	A.D. 632	A.D. 634
He was forced to flee to Medina (then Yathrib).	His flight from Mecca was so significant that this date became the first year in the Islamic calendar.	He made a triumphant entry into Mecca.	He died and was buried.	Abu Backer fought to reconvert the Arab tribes back to Islam (Ridda Wars).

MUHAMMAD, THE MESSENGER

In A.D. 610 Muhammad received his first _____ in which Allah revealed to him that he was a prophet.

According to Islamic tradition, an angel appeared to Muhammad and told him to recite. He had a spell and foamed at the mouth. Whatever he spoke was written down and later compiled into the Qur'an.

In A.D. 622 Muhammad was persecuted in Mecca, so he fled to Medina (an event known as Hijrah).

✣ Muhammad and his followers supported themselves by raiding passing caravans.

✣ In Medina, Muhammad rose as a political figure.

Muhammad finally conquered _____ in A.D. 630.

He destroyed the idols in the Ka'aba. As people converted to Islam, they were forced to speak Arabic, the language of the Qur'an.

Mu'awiya's victory divided Islam:
✣ Sunnis: leadership chosen through community consensus (followed the Sunnah)
✣ Shi'ites: leadership chosen through succession of imams

A.D. 642	A.D. 650	A.D. 656–661	A.D. 732
Iraq, Syria and Egypt fell into Muslim hands.	Uthman compiled the Qur'an and destroyed variant texts.	Internal fighting was waged between Ali and Mu'awiya.	Muslim army was defeated in the Battle of Tours.

In the gospel God's Word became Jesus. In Islam God's word became a book.

Islam Rising

SPREAD OF ISLAMIC ARMY

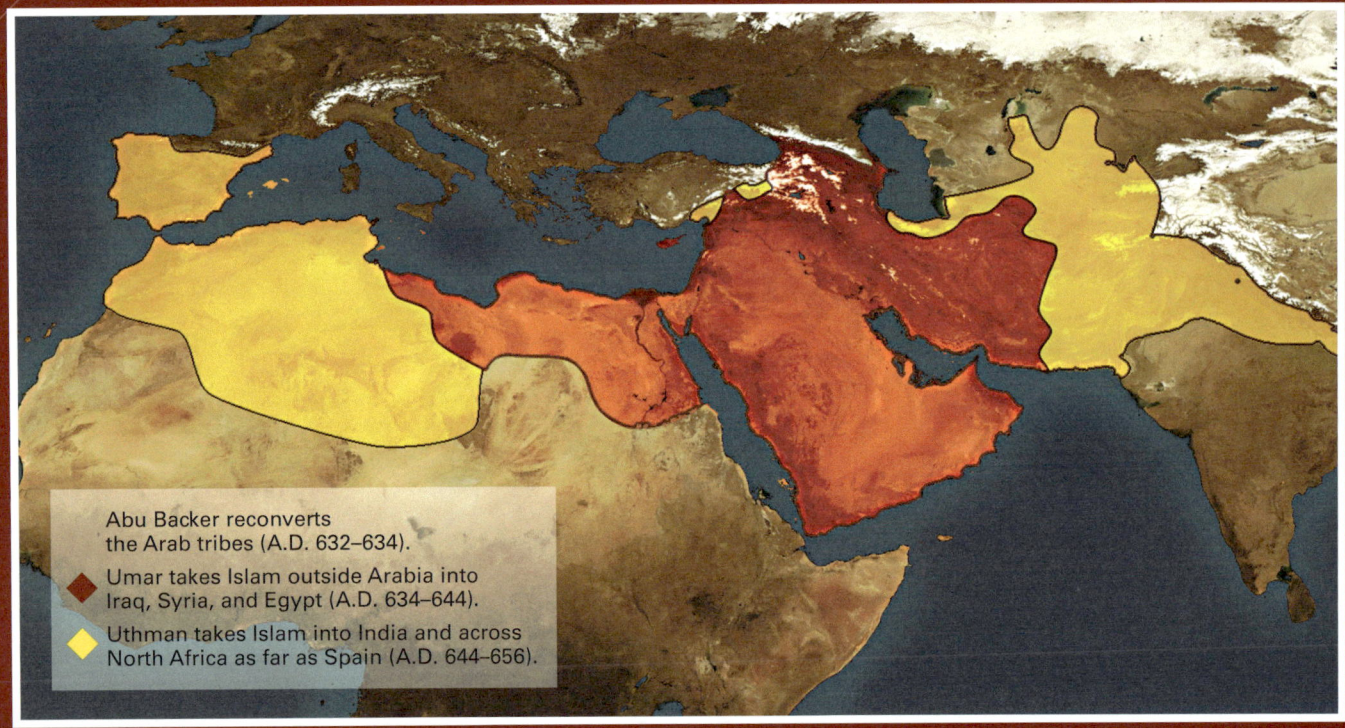

Abu Backer reconverts the Arab tribes (A.D. 632–634).

◆ Umar takes Islam outside Arabia into Iraq, Syria, and Egypt (A.D. 634–644).

◆ Uthman takes Islam into India and across North Africa as far as Spain (A.D. 644–656).

Positive things Muhammad accomplished:
1. United warring tribes
2. Abolished _____ _____
3. Gave more rights to _____
4. Stopped the practice of infanticide

QUR'AN

What is the Qur'an?
✤ The holy book of Islam
✤ Word of God revealed _____
   by _____ through Muhammad
✤ Arabic meaning = to recite

Importance
Muslims take the study of the Qur'an seriously. Some Muslims memorize the entire text.

The book itself is considered to have _____.

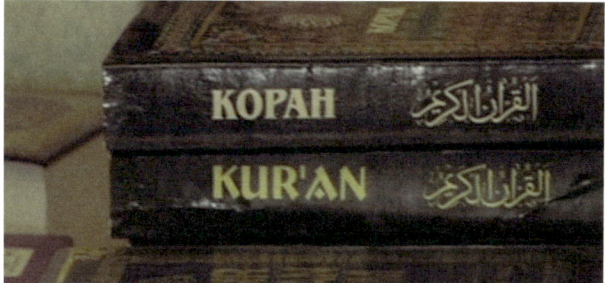

Muslim scholars say the Qur'an cannot be translated from Arabic, Allah's language. All attempts are translations of the "meaning" of the Qur'an.

HADITH

The Hadith are collected _____ of Muhammad, second only to the authority of the Qur'an. They were collected three hundred years after Muhammad's death.

Islam claims that the Hadith and the Qur'an must be studied together.

There are multiple versions of the Hadith (Sunni and Shi'ite have their own accounts).

THE QUR'AN TODAY
In approximately A.D. 650 Caliph Uthman bin Afan (the third caliph) compiled the first Qur'an from various writings of Muhammad's followers.

Uthman then burned all manuscripts and variant texts, leaving no original record available today.

ACTION

HOW CAN I MEET A MUSLIM?

Look online for Middle Eastern or Mediterranean restaurants because they are often run by Muslims. You can also find Muslim businesses near a mosque.

DISCUSS

What are two new things you learned about Islam today?

John 3:16 says God sent Jesus because of His love for the world. From what you know about Islam, what can Jesus offer Muslims?

MEMORIZE AND REFLECT

Read and memorize Matthew 24:14. What is your reaction to this verse?

ACTION ASSIGNMENT I: MAKE A MUSLIM FRIEND

1. Locate a Middle Eastern restaurant, shop, or market and try to meet someone who is a Muslim. Other places to meet a Muslim could include international festivals, work events, mosques, refugee centers, or ESL programs. (If you currently have a Muslim friend or neighbor, that's a great place to start.)
2. Begin a casual conversation with your new acquaintance. You could ask him what country he is from or about his family.
3. After you meet a Muslim, fill in the form on the next page.
4. Pray for your new Muslim friend by name daily.
5. Next week share about the experience with your group.

Matthew 24:14
"This good news of the kingdom will be proclaimed in all the world as a testimony to all nations. And then the end will come."

Date completed:

Tip: It is best for women to share with women and men to share with men.

For additional ideas and resources, visit
www.crescentproject.org
or *www.fouadmasri.com.*

New friend's name: _____

Where I met him/her: _____

Country of origin: _____

Contact information (if provided): _____

On a scale of 1 to 10, how nervous were you to approach him/her?

Totally at ease   **Scared to death**

1   2   3   4   5   6   7   8   9   10

How did Christ help you in this encounter?

_____

_____

_____

Bridges: Christians Connecting with Muslims

Belief and Ritual
SESSION 2

Psalm 119:160
"The entirety of Your word is truth, and all Your righteous judgments endure forever."

> **Colossians 2:13-14**
> "He made you alive with Him and forgave us all our trespasses. He erased the certificate of debt, with its obligations, that was against us and opposed to us, and has taken it out of the way by nailing it to the cross."

SESSION 2
BELIEF AND RITUAL

AFTER THIS SESSION YOU WILL UNDERSTAND:
✚ The basic belief system of Muslims.

✚ The rituals Muslims perform and the importance they hold.

✚ Some similarities and differences between Islam and Christianity.

PRAY:
✚ Your basic understanding of Muslims' beliefs will give you credibility in their eyes.

✚ By learning about Islamic rituals, you will be overcome with gratitude for the finished work of Christ (see Colossians 2:13-14)

✚ Your heart will be filled with Christ's compassion for Muslims.

Bridges: Christians Connecting with Muslims

DISCUSSION

Share what you learned from your Action Assignment. Did you meet a Muslim? What was your experience like?

WARM-UP

What is the difference between belief and ritual? List some of your Christian beliefs on the lines below. Next, list some Christian practices in which you participate.

BELIEF	RITUAL (OR PRACTICE)
_____	_____
_____	_____
_____	_____
_____	_____

Watch video session 2 and fill in the corresponding blanks.

Downloads of this book and video session can be purchased at *www.crescentproject.org* or *www.fouadmasri.com*.

VIDEO SESSION 2
BELIEF AND RITUAL

GOD IN THE QUR'AN

God in the Qur'an is not bound by his character; he is sovereign with the power to do both good and evil. God in the Bible is holy in His sovereignty.

BASIC ISLAMIC BELIEFS

1. BELIEF IN GOD

Allah means *only God* in Arabic.

99 BEAUTIFUL NAMES OF GOD:

God is known through His names.

In Islam you can be the best Muslim and not go to heaven because God can _____ _____ _____.

It is not the _____ of Allah with which we disagree; it is the _____ of Allah in Islam that contradicts God in the Bible.

Do not get caught up in semantics; Arabic speaking Christians also use *Allah* to refer to God.

2. BELIEF IN HIS ANGELS

In Islam God created sin, Satan, demons, angels, and Jinn.

✢ Angels are created from light to do good on earth.

✢ Demons are created from fire to do evil on earth.

✢ _____ are half human, half demonic. They tend to be regarded as demonic or controlled by Satan.

3. BELIEF IN HIS PROPHETS

Many of the prophets in Islam and Christianity are the same. Adam, Noah, Abraham, Moses, Jacob, Jesus, Job, Elijah, Jonah, and John the Baptist are all prophets in Islam.

Orthodox Islam teaches that Muhammad is the _____ (last) of the prophets.

4. BELIEF IN HIS BOOKS (OR MESSAGES)

Muslims must believe and follow the:

✢ Tawrat (Book of Moses).

✢ Zabur (Book of David).

✢ _____ (Book of Jesus or New Testament).

✢ Qur'an (Book of Muhammad).

Names that are not compatible with the biblical view of God:

* **Al Mumeet**
  The Source of death

* **Al Muntaqem**
  God will come after you out of vengeance, not necessarily justice

* **Al Macker**
  The Schemer; God can change his mind or scheme against you

Belief and Ritual

Rasul:
One who brings a message

Qur'an 2:136
"Say ye: 'We believe in Allah and the revelation given to us, and to Abraham, Isma`il, Isaac, Jacob, and the Tribes, and that given to Moses and Jesus, and that given to (all) Prophets from their Lord: We make no difference between one and another of them: And we bow to Allah (in Islam).'"

COMMON UNDERSTANDING

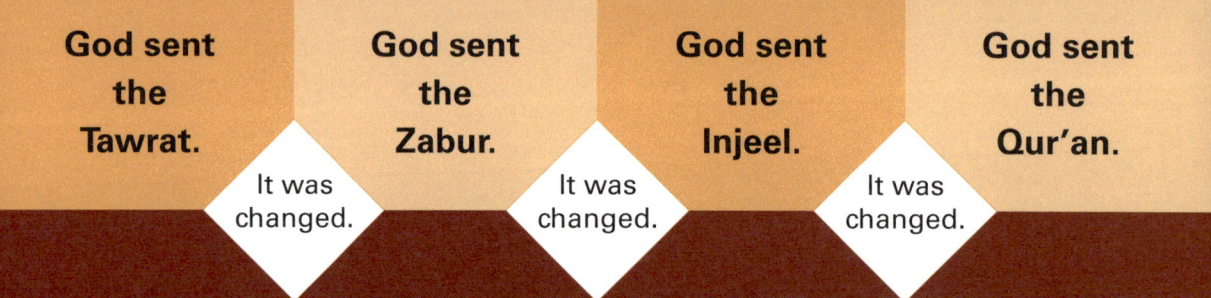

Most Muslims believe the Old and New Testaments have been _____ and are therefore not trustworthy. This teaching is not found in the Qur'an.

5. BELIEF IN THE LAST DAY OR JUDGMENT DAY

A scale will weigh the _____ and _____ deeds a person has committed; whichever deeds tip the scale determine the person's eternal destination—paradise or hell. However, Allah is not bound by these rules and can change his mind.

A MUSLIM VIEW OF...	
PARADISE	**HELL**
Four rivers: milk, honey, water, and wine	Perpetual fire
70 maidens take care of a man's physical needs.	Skin burns off, new skin is grown and burned off, and the cycle continues.
Very sensual	Traditional information borrowed from other religions
No mention of good Muslim women	Majority of dwellers are women.

Many of these views originate from various hadith.

1 John 1:9
"If we confess our sins, He is faithful and righteous to forgive us our sins and to cleanse us from all unrighteousness."

Fate: Another Core Belief of Muslims
Whatever Allah decrees—both good and bad—must come to pass.

Belief and Ritual

The Five Pillars of Islam

Creed (Al-Shahadah)

Prayer (Al-Salat)

Fasting (Al-Saum)

Alms Giving (Al-Zakat)

Pilgrimage (Al-Hajj)

PILLARS OF ISLAM

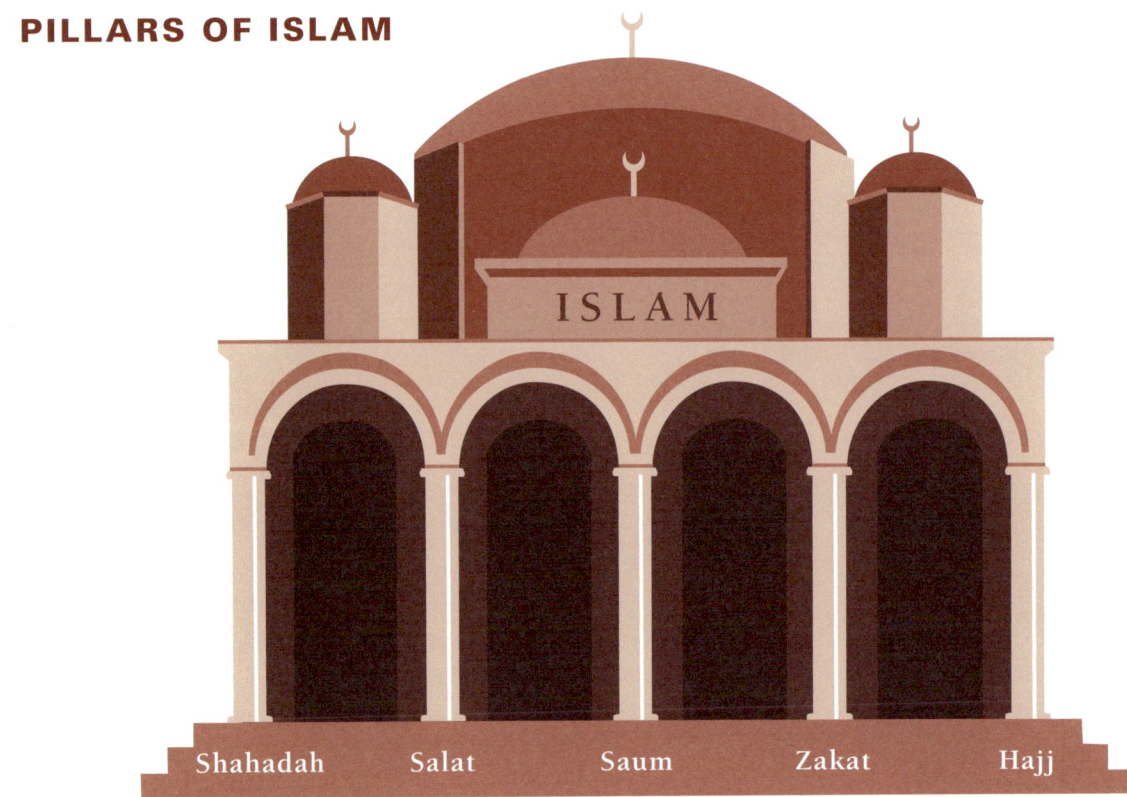

Bridges: Christians Connecting with Muslims

1. CREED (AL-SHAHADAH)

Creed: "I testify that there is no god except Allah, and I testify that Muhammad is the messenger of Allah."

Reciting this creed in the presence of a Muslim makes you a _____.

2. PRAYER (AL-SALAT)

A _____ _____ exercised in the mosque or alone five times a day.

It is a ritual, not a conversation with God. Communal prayers are regarded as good works.

Salat is different from Christian prayer, in which you can pray _____ or _____.

The five times of prayer:

1. Sunrise
2. Noon
3. Afternoon (usually two hours after the noon hour)
4. Sunset
5. Nighttime (usually two hours after sunset)

Muhammad ordered Muslims to pray toward Mecca instead of Jerusalem once they migrated to Medina.

Ablutions
Ritual _____ that must be done before prayers.

After performing ablutions, you cannot touch a woman or a non-Muslim (you become unclean).

3. FASTING (AL-SAUM)

During the month of Ramadan (when the first verses of the Qur'an were revealed), a Muslim is not allowed to eat as long as there is _____. However, Muslims make up the meals they miss during the day by _____ at night.

Inside the Mosque: Women and Men
Women must never pray in front of men in the mosque. Many husbands ask their wives to stay at home rather than go to the mosque.

Night of Destiny (Laylat al-Qadar)

- ✣ _____ night of Ramadan.
- ✣ _____ are answered on this night.
- ✣ Opportunity to change your destiny for the year
- ✣ Some Muslims stay up all night reading the Qur'an.

4. ALMSGIVING (AL-ZAKAT)

The percentage of a Muslim's wealth given as alms to needy Muslims

_____ Sunni

_____ Shi'ite

Muslims depend on their religious leaders to determine the precise amount.

5. PILGRIMAGE (AL-HAJJ)

Pilgrimage to Mecca and Medina that must be made by every able Muslim at least _____ in his _____

During the Hajj a pilgrim circles the Ka'aba seven times and attempts to touch or kiss the Ka'aba's black stone.

Muhammad circled the Ka'aba before Islam. Tradition says Abraham built the Ka'aba to sacrifice his son.

A Muslim who has completed the Hajj is given the respected title of Hajji.

Belief and Ritual

ACTION

DISCUSS

Injeel (in-JEEL): the Book of Jesus (New Testament)

Tawrat (tawr-AHT): the Book of Moses (name usually given to the entire Old Testament except Psalms)

Zabur (zuh-BUR): the Book of David (Psalms)

Why do you think memorizing Scripture from the Injeel, Tawrat, and Zabur might be helpful in sharing with Muslims?

_____

_____

_____

MEMORIZE AND REFLECT

From the book of David (Zabur), memorize and meditate on Psalm 119:160.

From the book of Moses (Tawrat), memorize and reflect on Deuteronomy 6:4-7.

From the book of Jesus (Injeel), memorize and reflect on Mark 13:31.

Psalm 119:160
"The entirety of Your word is truth, and all Your righteous judgments endure forever."

Belief and Ritual

ACTION ASSIGNMENT 2: LEARN ABOUT A MUSLIM HOLIDAY

1. This week initiate another conversation with your Muslim friend.

2. During the course of a conversation, ask him to explain some traditions or holidays he observes and their importance. You might say, "I'm curious about what holidays you celebrate. What is your most important celebration?"

3. Be prepared to answer a reciprocal question from your friend. He may ask you about the meaning behind a Christian holiday like Christmas or Easter.

Which holiday did your Muslim friend explain to you? _____

Why was this celebration important to him/her? _____

Was there any aspect of the holiday that caught your attention or could serve as a bridge to the gospel or a way to introduce Jesus?   ❏ Yes   ❏ No

If so, what? _____

_____

_____

Date completed:

Bridges: Christians Connecting with Muslims

Attitudes of an Ambassador
SESSION 3

2 Corinthians 5:20
"We are ambassadors for Christ, certain that God is appealing through us."

Ephesians 4:15
"Speaking the truth in love, let us grow in every way into Him who is the head—Christ."

SESSION 3
ATTITUDES OF AN AMBASSADOR

AFTER THIS SESSION YOU WILL BE ABLE TO:
✢ Share with Muslims in a correct state of heart.
✢ Identify three general types of Muslims.
✢ Learn keys to initiating natural relationships with Muslims.

PRAY GOD WILL EMPOWER YOU WITH:
✢ Wise actions that glorify God among Muslims (see Colossians 4:5).
✢ Speech that is respectful toward Muslims (see Colossians 4:6).
✢ A heart of an ambassador in your interactions (see 2 Corinthians 5:20).

Bridges: Christians Connecting with Muslims

WARM-UP

What are some tense subjects that could arise in a conversation with a Muslim?

✢ _____

✢ _____

✢ _____

Could these topics be avoided? If not, how could they be handled?

_____

_____

_____

_____

Watch video session 3 and fill in the corresponding blanks.

Downloads of this book and video session can be purchased at *www.crescentproject.org* or *www.fouadmasri.com*.

Attitudes of an Ambassador

Matthew 28:18-20
"Jesus came near and said to them, 'All authority has been given to Me in heaven and on earth. Go, therefore, and make disciples of all nations, baptizing them in the name of the Father and of the Son and of the Holy Spirit, teaching them to observe everything I have commanded you. And remember, I am with you always, to the end of the age.'"

2 Corinthians 5:20
"We are ambassadors for Christ, certain that God is appealing through us. We plead on Christ's behalf, 'Be reconciled to God.'"

AMBASSADORS

What is an ambassador?

✝ _____ his country

✝ Our job is to _____.
God makes people Christians, not us.

FOUR ATTITUDES

LOVING
Show unconditional compassion.

We came to Christ because we saw Christ's love in others.

FRIENDLY
✝ Build a friendship.

✝ Do not _____ Muslim beliefs.

✝ Do not _____.

BRIDGING
Bridge the Gospel
Take the _____ concepts of Islam and Christianity and build a bridge. Start building a bridge and pray your friend will step out in faith to cross it.

BIBLICAL
✝ Always use the Bible.

✝ Give the Injeel (New Testament) as a gift.

Note:
Because many Muslims are taught negative and incorrect information about Christianity, it often takes a genuine relationship and sufficient time to correct these false assumptions and to present the truth.

Most Muslims will hear the gospel many times before they believe; you may be a link in the chain of people representing Christ to one person.

Attitudes of an Ambassador

The best gift we can give is the Injeel, the Word of God.

TYPES OF MUSLIMS
CULTURAL

✢ Constitute the majority of the Muslims worldwide, representing all classes of society and countless ethnic groups

✢ They have only _____ information about Islam and therefore do not normally adhere to and perform all of the rituals.

✢ They are open to hearing the gospel and to considering the lordship of Jesus Christ.

CONVERTS

✢ From a variety of backgrounds

✢ Ask them, "Why did you become Muslim?"

DEVOUT

✢ May be well informed about their religion and able to discuss Islam with an open mind

✢ Highly involved in the religious rituals, but some may have no formal education

✢ Show love and understanding to them rather than an argumentative spirit, even though they might tend to argue.

Remember
Be patient.
Wait on the Lord
for the timing
and opportunities
to share.

Answer criticism
if necessary in
order to correct
false information
about Christ and
Christianity.

Give the Injeel
as a gift.

Expect results.

APPROACH

1. Pray.

2. Build friendships.

3. Present your faith in a _____ manner. Muslims are very open to discussing spiritual issues.

4. Smile to keep the conversation relaxed.

5. Witness one-on-one when possible.

ACTION

2 Corinthians 5:20
"We are ambassadors for Christ, certain that God is appealing through us."

MEMORIZE AND REFLECT

Read and memorize 2 Corinthians 5:20.

DISCUSS

From what you know about your friend, how would you describe him?

❏ **Cultural**—His religion is based on traditional beliefs; he is Muslim because his parents were Muslim.

❏ **Convert**—He converted to the religion from another background.

❏ **Devout**—He is highly involved in religious rituals and is knowledgeable about Islam.

What approach do you think will be best to take with your friend?

_____
_____
_____
_____

Bridges: Christians Connecting with Muslims

ACTION ASSIGNMENT 3: PRAY FOR MUSLIMS

One of our core values at Crescent Project is a concerted prayer effort.

This week take time each day (at least five minutes) praying for your Muslim friend by name. You can also pray for Muslims around the world, but try to focus your prayer on one specific individual or family you know.

You can pray for:

- Workers to be sent to the harvest in the Muslim world. Only 7 percent of missionaries are working among Muslims; that means there are approximately three workers for every one million Muslims.
- Muslims to recognize Christ's uniqueness among the prophets. Pray they will read the Book of Jesus—the Injeel—and have faith to believe.
- God's revelation in your Muslim friend's heart. Many Muslims who come to faith in Christ are stirred to believe through dreams and visions of Jesus. Pray God will manifest His power, presence, and provision on their behalf.

"Our job is not to make a Muslim become a Christian. Our job is to show them the love of Christ."
—Fouad Masri

Call to Prayer
Call to Prayer is a biweekly e-mail from Fouad Masri that helps you pray effectively for Muslims.

Subscribe online at *www.crescentproject.org/prayer*.

Date completed:

What is the name of the Muslim you prayed for this week? _____

What specific requests did you have?
_____
_____

As you have prayed for Muslims, did any of your attitudes change?
_____
_____

How is prayer affecting your faith and actions?
_____
_____

Bridging the Gospel
SESSION 4

2 Corinthians 2:14
"Thanks be to God, who always puts us on display in Christ and through us spreads the aroma of the knowledge of Him in every place."

SESSION 4
BRIDGING THE GOSPEL

AFTER THIS SESSION YOU WILL UNDERSTAND:
✢ The basic similarities and differences between Islam and Christianity.

✢ How some Muslim beliefs can serve as bridges to the gospel.

✢ How to communicate the truth of Jesus' life, death, and resurrection to a Muslim.

PRAY:
✢ You will better understand the gospel of Jesus in contrast to what Muslims believe.

✢ This understanding will help build bridges of truth to Muslims.

Bridges: Christians Connecting with Muslims

WARM-UP

What are four attitudes that should characterize your interactions with Muslims?

Four Attitudes of an Ambassador

1. _____

2. _____

3. _____

4. _____

DISCUSSION

From what you know about Islam so far, what, in your opinion, is the biggest difference between Islam and Christianity?

_____

_____

_____

Watch video session 4 and fill in the corresponding blanks.

BASIC SIMILARITIES
GOD IS ONE
Both Muslims and Christians believe in one God.

Names of God that Muslims and Christians agree on:

✢ Al-Barry = the Creator

✢ Al-Qudoos = _____

✢ Al-Raheem = _____

✢ Al-Malek = the King

MAN IS SINFUL

✢ While Muslims believe everyone sins, they do not believe in _____ _____. (It is better to focus on people being sinners rather than on Adam's sin.)

✢ Prophets (including Muhammad) sin and fall short of God's law, according to the Qur'an.

✢ Jesus was the only sinless prophet.

✢ Sin = not meeting God's righteous standards

JESUS CHRIST
Muslims believe Jesus:

✢ Was born of the _____

✢ Was conceived by the power of God

✢ Is the _____ ____ _____ (Kalimat Allah—no difference between God and His Word)

✢ Was pure and sinless from birth

✢ Raised the dead and healed the sick

✢ Will be the _____ on Judgment Day

✢ Is coming back to earth

> **Qur'an 4:171**
> "Christ Jesus the son of Mary was (no more than) an apostle of Allah, and His Word, which He bestowed on Mary, and a spirit proceeding from Him."

Note: Although the Qur'an agrees with the Bible that Jesus is the Word of God and the Spirit of God, Islamic leaders teach he was just a man who was never crucified and will return to earth someday.

More names of God that Christians and Muslims agree on:

✱ Al-Adil = the Just

✱ Al-Wadud = the Affectionate

Bridging the Gospel

HOLY BOOKS

1. Tawrat—first five books of the Old Testament
2. Zabur—the Psalms
3. Injeel—New Testament, the Book of Jesus

Christians look at all other religions through the lens of the New Testament.

PROPHETS

- Adam
- Noah
- Abraham (God redeemed the son of Abraham with a ram. Muslims call this the Adha sacrifice.)
- Jonah
- John the Baptist

WHAT THE BIBLE SAYS ABOUT JESUS

John 1:1
"In the beginning was the Word, and the Word was with God, and the Word was God."

John 1:14
"The Word became flesh and and took up residence among us. We observed His glory, the glory as the One and Only Son from the Father, full of grace and truth."

Hebrews 1:1-2
"Long ago God spoke to the fathers by the prophets at different times and in different ways. In these last days, He has spoken to us by His Son. God has appointed Him heir of all things and made the universe through Him."

Bridges: Christians Connecting with Muslims

BASIC DIFFERENCES

THE SONSHIP OF JESUS

Muslims are taught that Christians believe Mary had a _____ _____ with God.

TRINITY

Muslims think Christians worship three gods—God, Jesus, and Mary.

Christians believe in a complex One, while Muslims believe in a simple One.

CRUCIFIXION AND RESURRECTION OF JESUS

According to Muslim logic, if Christ was a prophet sent from God, He should _____ and not lose by dying.

Muslims interpret the Qur'an to say that Christ was not really killed but taken up into heaven.

AUTHORITY OF THE BIBLE

Muslims believe that the Bible has been _____.

Muslims believe the Qur'an replaces the Bible.

The Qur'an tells Muslims to read the Tawrat, Zabur, and Injeel.

The Qur'an says Christians have the power to judge the message of the Qur'an.

SALVATION BY GRACE

Muslims believe that they take _____ for their sins, while Christians just _____ them to Christ.

Address the differences. Focus on the similarities.

The Five Pillars of Christianity

* One God
* One Savior
* One Spirit
* One message
* One family

Bridging the Gospel

ACTION

DISCUSS

2 Corinthians 2:14-15

"Thanks be to God, who always puts us on display in Christ and through us spreads the aroma of the knowledge of Him in every place. For to God we are the fragrance of Christ among those who are being saved and among those who are perishing."

According to 2 Corinthians 2:14-15, what fragrance does a follower of Christ bring?

_____

How can you be the aroma of Christ among Muslims this week?

_____

MEMORIZE AND REFLECT

Read and memorize 2 Corinthians 2:14-15.

What does it mean to be the fragrance, or aroma, of Christ?

_____

_____

_____

Date completed:

ACTION ASSIGNMENT 4: SHARE A MEAL

One major biblical value is hospitality, sharing a meal. Many Muslims hold this same value as Christians. They believe sharing a meal with someone creates a bond between two persons similar to that within a family. If you share a meal with someone, you are bound to that person through the exchanging of favors. A meal in many ways "seals the deal" of friendship.

Meet your Muslim friend for a meal at a restaurant of her choice. Continue building the friendship. Know that by sharing a meal, you are not only eating together but also creating a bond of friendship.

How would you best describe your stage of friendship with a Muslim?

❏ Awkward and distant   ❏ Warm and open

❏ Friendly but guarded   ❏ Like family

❏ Trust building   ❏ Other _____

From what you know about your friend's life, what does he or she:

Value? _____

Need? _____

Fear? _____

What is halal?
Some Muslims are particular about food choices and eat only halal, or foods prepared according to Islamic dietary laws. In this case your friend may prefer to eat at a halal restaurant. Other Muslims aren't concerned about halal foods but abstain from pork products and alcohol.

Bridges: Christians Connecting with Muslims

Tools for Reaching Muslims
Understanding the New Testament's Credibility

SESSION 5

Mark 13:31
"Heaven and earth will pass away, but My words will never pass away."

Isaiah 55:11
"My word that comes from My mouth will not return to Me empty, but it will accomplish what I please and will prosper in what I send it to do."

SESSION 5
TOOLS FOR REACHING MUSLIMS
UNDERSTANDING THE NEW TESTAMENT'S CREDIBILITY

AFTER THIS SESSION YOU WILL BE ABLE TO:
✢ Answer the most common question Muslims have about Christianity.
✢ Share about the authenticity of the Injeel (New Testament) in a sensitive way.
✢ Present theological, logical, and historical reasoning for the Injeel's integrity.

PRAY GOD WILL:
✢ Increase your confidence in the Bible's credibility.
✢ Give you natural opportunities to share God's Word with Muslims.
✢ Release His Word among Muslims in a way that does not return to Him empty but accomplishes the purposes for which He sent it (see Isaiah 55:11).

Bridges: Christians Connecting with Muslims

WARM-UP

From your experience so far, is it easy to befriend Muslims?   ❏ Yes   ❏ No

What is the most helpful advice you have received in building relationships with Muslims?

_____

_____

_____

_____

_____

Watch video session 5 and fill in the corresponding blanks.

Downloads of this book and video session can be purchased at *www.crescentproject.org* or *www.fouadmasri.com*.

VIDEO SESSION 5
UNDERSTANDING THE NEW TESTAMENT'S CREDIBILITY

AUTHENTICITY OF THE INJEEL

The Muslim says:

"Hasn't the Injeel been corrupted?"

"Isn't the Qur'an the replacement for the Injeel?"

Though most Muslims have never read it for themselves, they claim the Injeel has been corrupted. We need to come to the heart of the issue in Muslim evangelism: the Bible is trustworthy and should be followed. Apologetics is a way to lift the veil of misunderstanding about the Injeel so that Muslims will read it for themselves.

Qur'an 2:146
"The people of the Book know this as they know their own sons; but some of them conceal the truth which they themselves know."

Qur'an 2:136
"Say ye: 'We believe in Allah, and the revelation given to us, and to Abraham, Isma'il, Isaac, Jacob, and the Tribes, and that given to Moses and Jesus, and that given to (all) prophets from their Lord: We make no difference between one and another of them: And we bow to Allah (in Islam).'"

Qur'an 3:2-3
"Allah! There is no god but He, the Living, the Self-Subsisting, Eternal. It is He Who sent down to thee (step by step), in truth, the Book, **confirming what went before it;** and He sent down the Law (of Moses) and the Gospel (of Jesus) before this, as a guide to mankind."

Understanding the New Testament's Credibility

COMMON UNDERSTANDING

God sent the Tawrat.

It was changed.

God sent the Zabur.

It was changed.

God sent the Injeel.

It was changed.

God sent the Qur'an.

COMMON MUSLIM UNDERSTANDING

✟ The Tawrat of Moses was corrupted, so God sent the Zabur.

✟ The Zabur of David was corrupted, so God sent the Injeel.

✟ The Injeel of Jesus was corrupted, so God sent the Qur'an.

✟ The Qur'an will never be changed since God protects His word.

Islamic leaders (imams) teach:

✟ The Injeel has gone through many versions, and the real _____ has been lost.

✟ Christians have changed many stories and deleted any references to Islam and Muhammad. This accusation is not backed by research.

2 Timothy 3:16-17
"All Scripture is inspired by God and is profitable for teaching, for rebuking, for correcting, for training in righteousness, so that the man of God may be complete, equipped for every good work."

CHRISTIAN PERSPECTIVE

✟ God inspired the writing of the Injeel.

✟ God will keep His Word to enlighten and _____ the human race.

✟ The many versions are merely translations with the same message.

✟ Interested individuals may learn Koine Greek and study the Injeel in the original language.

Respond on three levels:

✸ Theological
✸ Logical
✸ Historical

Understanding the New Testament's Credibility

What does the Qur'an say about the Injeel?

Qur'an 3:2-3
2:136
57:27
5:47
5:68

APPROACH

Mark 13:31

"Heaven and earth will pass away, but My words will never pass away."

1. Theological

When Muslims say the Bible has been corrupted, respond with "Astaghfurallah!" (_____).

If a person believes the Injeel is corrupted, he or she believes _____ are stronger than God.

God promised in the Injeel to keep His Word.

God must keep His Word so that He will be a just judge.

2. Logical

An objective look at whether the Injeel has been corrupted must answer these questions:

✢ Who corrupted the Injeel?
✢ Why was the Injeel corrupted?
✢ Where was the Injeel corrupted?
✢ _____ was the Injeel corrupted?
✢ _____ is the original Injeel?
✢ What parts of the Injeel were corrupted?
✢ Was the Injeel corrupted _____ or _____ the life of Muhammad?

Islam does not answer these questions, so we need to help our Muslim friend take a closer look at the history of the Injeel.

Bridges: Christians Connecting with Muslims

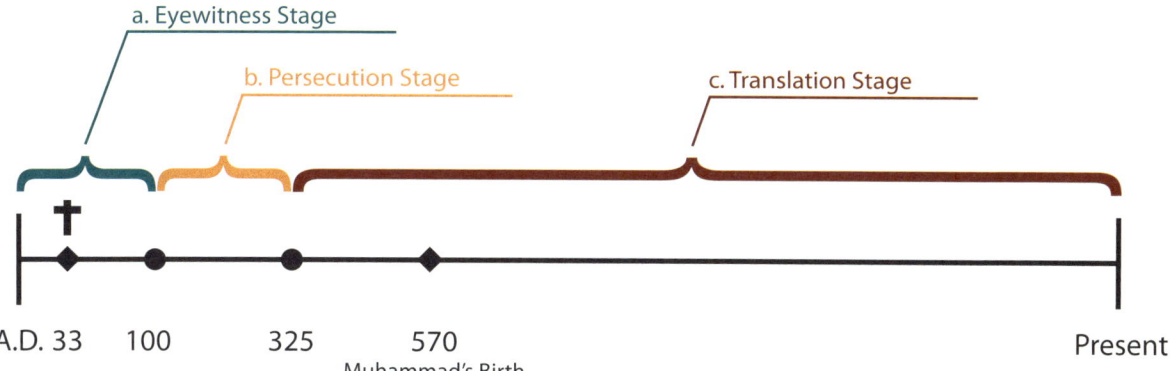

3. Historical

The following is a historical overview of the manuscript record of the Injeel (New Testament) from A.D. 0 to the present.

a. The Eyewitness Stage (A.D. 1–100)

✛ A.D. 33: Jesus Christ of Nazareth was crucified and raised from the dead.

✛ A.D. 100: There are no _____ _____ of the life, crucifixion, and resurrection of Jesus.

b. The Persecution Stage (A.D. 100–325)

✛ The Romans decreed to martyr Christians and burn their books.

✛ Partial manuscripts were found.

✛ Writings/letters of church fathers

✛ Lectionaries

✛ Early translations

Understanding the New Testament's Credibility

THREE-LEVEL APPROACH

✛ **Theologically**, God keeps His Word to enlighten us.

✛ **Logically**, no one can answer these questions.

✛ **Historically**, the Bible has not been changed.

c. **The Translation Stage (A.D. 325–Present)**

✢ A.D. 325: Codex Sinaiticus, found in Saint Catherine's Monastery on Mount Sinai

✢ A.D. 350: Codex Vaticanus, in the Vatican

✢ A.D. 400: Codex Alexandrinus, found in Alexandria, Egypt

✢ All present-day translations are based on the Greek manuscripts. The message is one, and the meaning is the same.

✢ There are manuscripts available prior to Muhammad's birth in A.D. 570. Muhammad instructed Muslims to believe and therefore read the Injeel as part of following Islam.

POINT OF DECISION

Revelation 3:20
"Listen! I stand at the door and knock. If anyone hears My voice and opens the door, I will come in to him and have dinner with him, and he with Me."

1. Use the bridge as a thermometer. With some Muslims you will need to use the whole bridge, while others will need only parts.

2. You may need to relay information more than once because some will not grasp this the first time.

3. By pointing Muslims to the authenticity of the Injeel, you bring them to the heart of the gospel—that Jesus lived, was crucified, and rose from the dead.

Q: Who is stronger—God or humans?

A: God is stronger.

Luke 1:37
"Nothing will be impossible with God."

Qur'an 2:148
"Allah has power over all things."

Understanding the New Testament's Credibility

DISCUSS

What does Fouad mean when he says, "Use the bridge as a thermometer"? In what situations do you think sharing only parts of the bridge may be most helpful?

_____

_____

MEMORIZE AND REFLECT

Read and memorize Mark 13:31. Why will God's Word never pass away?

_____

_____

In Islam God's word became a book. Muslims believe the Qur'an was sent down as an exact replica of a Golden Qur'an preserved in heaven. How do 2 Timothy 3:16, Hebrews 4:12, and John 1:14 present different views of God's Word as living and active?

_____

_____

John 1:14
"The Word became flesh and took up residence among us. We observed His glory, the glory as the One and Only Son from the Father, full of grace and truth."

Mark 13:31
"Heaven and earth will pass away, but My words will never pass away."

ACTION ASSIGNMENT 5: SHARE THE INJEEL

Invite your Muslim friend to join you for tea or coffee and pray for an opening to share Scripture or give the Injeel (New Testament) to her as a gift. Some ways you can open the way for a discussion about the Injeel are:

✢ Listen to your friend's concerns or fears and share a teaching or parable of Jesus that ministers to her need. Ask her if she's ever read the New Testament, or the Book of Jesus.

✢ If your friend mentions the Qur'an, ask if she knows what her book says about the Injeel. Ask her if she'd like a copy of the Injeel to read for herself.

✢ She may ask for advice about a family situation or what your opinion is of a political issue. Be prepared to share Scripture that addresses the particular issue and encourage her to read the Injeel for herself.

Did you have an opportunity to talk about the Injeel with your friend?   ❑ Yes   ❑ No
If yes, what did the conversation center on?

✢ Integrity of the Injeel
✢ Jesus' teachings
✢ Other: _____.
✢ Qur'an replacing other books
✢ How the New Testament addresses social issues

On a scale of 1 to 10, how interested is your friend in spiritual matters?

Not interested at all   **Seriously seeking truth**

1   2   3   4   5   6   7   8   9   10

Bridges: Christians Connecting with Muslims

Date completed:

You can order the Injeel in common Muslim languages at Crescent Project's online resource center. Go online to www.crescentproject.org/resources.

Tools for Reaching Muslims
Understanding Jesus' Sacrifice

SESSION 6

1 John 1:9
"If we confess our sins, He is faithful and righteous to forgive us our sins and to cleanse us from all unrighteousness."

SESSION 6
TOOLS FOR REACHING MUSLIMS
UNDERSTANDING JESUS' SACRIFICE

AFTER THIS SESSION YOU WILL BE ABLE TO:
- Understand why Muslims think grace is a ticket for immorality.
- Share how Jesus did not lose by dying.
- Explain how Christ became the true Adha (sacrifice).

PRAY:
- You will grasp the meaning in Abraham's willingness to sacrifice his son.
- Muslims will be aware of their sin and need for a Savior.
- For openings to share this truth with your Muslim friend.

WARM-UP

What would you say to a Muslim who says the Injeel is corrupted? How would you begin? How could you use the three parts of the bridge (theological, logical, and historical)?

_____

_____

_____

_____

Watch video session 6 and fill in the corresponding blanks.

Downloads of this book and video session can be purchased at *www.crescentproject.org* or *www.fouadmasri.com*.

Understanding Jesus' Sacrifice

VIDEO SESSION 6

UNDERSTANDING JESUS' SACRIFICE

SALVATION BY GRACE

Typical comments from Muslims:

"Why did Jesus have to die?"

"Since Jesus is a prophet, how can He lose by dying?"

"There is no need for sacrifice. Aren't we saved through good works? Christians are lazy and don't take care of their sins. Good Muslims take ownership for their sins and work to take care of them."

Qur'an 7:8-9
"The balance that day will be true (to nicety): those whose scale (of good) will be heavy, will prosper: Those whose scale will be light, will be their souls in perdition, for that they have wrongfully treated Our signs."

Understanding Jesus' Sacrifice

Acts 4:12
"There is salvation in no one else, for there is no other name under heaven given to people, and we must be saved by it."

COMMON MUSLIM UNDERSTANDING

1. Christians are lazy and morally loose. They sin, and Jesus just keeps forgiving.

2. Christianity is _____ in punishing Jesus for the sins of others.

3. Muslims pride themselves in righteous acts that will _____ sins on Judgment Day.

Religious leaders teach:

1. God is a just _____ _____. He is a great businessman; you cannot steal from Him.

2. God punishes each person according to his/her sins, and punishing Jesus for others is not just.

3. Life is a test, and on Judgment Day your individual _____ _____ will get you into paradise.

CHRISTIAN PERSPECTIVE

Ephesians 2:8-9
"You are saved by grace through faith, and this is not from yourselves; it is God's gift—not from works, so that no one can boast."

✥ God is holy, and all humans are sinful. No one is righteous in the sight of God.

✥ All humans have already failed the righteousness test.

✥ God is a just judge. A _____ cannot redeem another _____.

✥ Jesus Christ was sinless from birth. He conquered sin, death, and Satan and therefore can intercede for humanity.

✥ Jesus is the true Adha sacrifice. He paid the debt we owe to God.

✥ Forgiveness can be experienced when we come to God through the redemption of Christ.

Bridges: Christians Connecting with Muslims

APPROACH

1. Ask, "What if the scale on Judgment Day is _____?"
2. Share that all of us need a redeemer to save us from the _____ and _____ of sin. Introduce the concept of grace.

Share about God's character:

✢ God is love (Al Wadud—the Affectionate).

✢ God is holy (Al Qudoos—the Holy One).

✢ God is just (Al Adil—the Just).

✢ God is merciful (Al Raheem—the Merciful).

✢ God is forgiving (Al Ghafoor—the Forgiver).

Christ the Eternal Sacrifice:

✢ Christ is _____ in His birth.

✢ Christ is sinless.

✢ Christ performed miracles.

✢ Christ _____ the whole universe.

✢ Christ rose from the dead, conquering sin, death, and Satan.

✢ Christ became the true Adha.

Hebrews 10:12
"This man, after offering one sacrifice for sins forever, sat down at the right hand of God."

POINT OF DECISION

1. Repent *(Toub)*
   Repentance is turning away from sin and focusing on God.

2. Confess or _____ *(Ish-had)*
   Confess that Jesus is your only Savior from the penalty and power of sin.

Muslim
"I hope the mercy of God will tip the scale of the good."

John 1:17
"The law was given through Moses, grace and truth came through Jesus Christ."

Understanding Jesus' Sacrifice

ACTION

DISCUSS

In pairs take turns sharing and explaining the concept of salvation by grace as if you were sharing it with a Muslim. Use concepts you've learned from this lesson. (For additional insight read *Adha in the Injeel*, available at the back of this study book, beginning on p. 133). It is an evangelistic tool that explains to a Muslim the necessity of Christ's sacrifice.

MEMORIZE AND REFLECT

Read and memorize 1 John 1:9.

Why might salvation by grace be a confusing concept to some Muslims? Why would it be freeing to others?

_____

_____

_____

_____

_____

1 John 1:9
"If we confess our sins, He is faithful and righteous to forgive us our sins and to cleanse us from all unrighteousness."

ACTION ASSIGNMENT 6: SHARE ABOUT JESUS' SACRIFICE

Meet with your Muslim friend again. Pray for God to open the door to discuss Jesus' great sacrifice. Use this time to continue building your relationship. Present the information with conviction and with sincerity, but try not to argue. Instead, bring the conversation back to Jesus Christ. Pray God will give you discernment and sensitivity in your interactions.

After understanding Muslim beliefs in depth, what aspect of Christianity do you have a greater appreciation for?

_____

_____

_____

Did you hold any misconceptions about Islam and Muslims that were challenged in this study or by meeting a Muslim? If so, what were they?

_____

_____

_____

Date completed:

Share *Adha in the Injeel* with your friend. Order the booklet or an outreach gift pack at www.crescentproject.org/bookstore.

Next Steps

NEXT STEPS

You made it! I'm so glad you were up to the challenge of learning about Islam and how to relate to Muslims as Christ would. I hope you've already put your training into practice through a friendship with a Muslim.

But what's next? I believe you were a part of this Bridges *study for a reason. God didn't give you this training so that you could slide it neatly on a shelf. Instead, He desires to use what you learned to grow you in Christ, spread His kingdom among Muslims, and share this teaching with other Christians.*

PRAY WITH US: CALL TO PRAYER

This biweekly prayer e-mail will keep you updated on events in the Muslim world, as well as direct you to pray for Muslims you know on Fridays at noon. Read stories of changed lives and of Christians who are reaching beyond themselves to share the gospel with Muslims in North America. Subscribe to Call to Prayer at *www.crescentproject.org/prayer*.

REACH OUT: OUTREACH TEAMS

After completing the *Bridges* study, your group has the unique opportunity to form an Outreach Team. Learn the benefits of being a part of an Outreach Team at *www.crescentproject.org/oasisteams*.

DIGGING DEEPER: OASIS CONFERENCE

If you want to dig deeper, Oasis Conference is the place to do it! Oasis Conference is a chance for Christians to network together and receive practical training and resources for equipping their church to reach out to Muslims. There will also be a chance to meet Muslim-background believers, visit a mosque, and attend various workshops. Go to *www.crescentproject.org/oasis* for more information.

INTENSIVE TRAINING: SAHARA CHALLENGE

Sahara Challenge is an intense week of training for participants who want to deepen their passion and expand their knowledge of Muslim ministry. Once you've completed the training, optional overseas and stateside mission trips are available. Visit *www.crescentproject.org/sahara* to learn more.

MEET MUSLIMS: SHORT-TERM TRIPS

Come face-to-face with Muslims on a two-week trip to the Muslim world. Join us as we live among the local people, strike up conversations on campuses and in crowded markets, and witness firsthand how God is at work among Muslims. Find specific trip options at *www.crescentproject.org/trips*.

Crescent Project is here to serve you. Please write or call today and let us know how God is opening doors in your city to reach out to Muslims with the compassion of Christ.

info@crescentproject.org
(888) 446-5457

Sahara Challenge

www.crescentproject.org/sahara

Mission trips and week-long, intensive training that will prepare you for effective ministry!

crescent project
HOPE WORTH SHARING

Oasis Conference

www.crescentproject.org/oasis

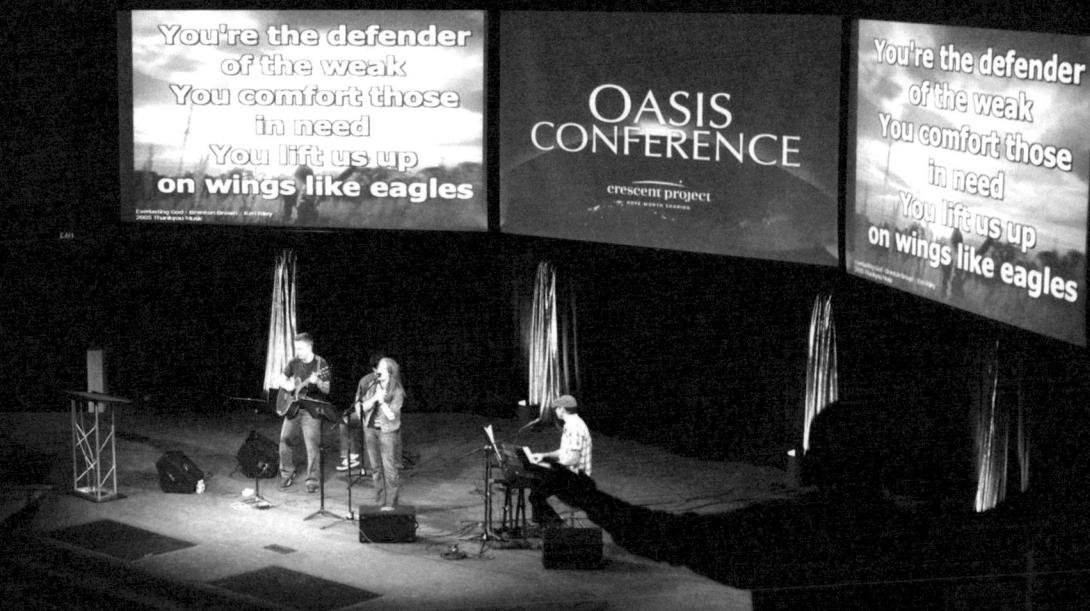

A national convention with renowned speakers.
A must for anyone interested in Muslim outreach!

crescent project
HOPE WORTH SHARING

Leader's Notes

Dear Bridges Leader:

Thank you for joining us on the Bridges journey and leading a small group through this inspirational and practical study! We want to assist you in every way to make your leadership experience the best possible.

The Bridges DVD Small-Group Study is made up of six 60-minute group sessions and outside fieldwork called Action Assignments. In addition to the hour of group session time each week, you will need approximately one to two hours of preparation outside class for your group to have the maximum benefit from Bridges.

E-mail us at info@crescentproject.org with any questions.

PREPARATION (ONE TO TWO HOURS)

Each group member will have the opportunity to complete an Action Assignment between sessions. We encourage you to complete these assignments along with your group. In addition, you will want to prepare for leading the coming session in the following ways.

- ✢ **Watch the Video Session** *to gain a deeper understanding of the material. Make notes to share with your group.*
- ✢ **Review the discussion questions** *for the coming session and prepare your own answers. Be sure to use the suggested answers listed in the Leader's Notes.*
- ✢ **Review the Scripture-memory assignment** *for the coming session; memorize it and be ready to discuss its importance.*
- ✢ **Review the Action Assignment** *and extra information or tips included in your Leader's Notes.*
- ✢ **Pray for each group member by name,** *and ask God to give you wisdom to lead them.*

LEADING THE SESSION (ONE HOUR)

Each session follows a similar format but can be adjusted to your specific group's needs. A general session outline follows:

- Prayer
- Warm-up
- Video Session
- Discussion
- Action Assignment

The order and components of each session are designed to guide your group into new and sometimes difficult material. Your presence and encouragement during each session will be crucial to the perseverance of your group members.

WHAT'S NEXT?

Your Bridges group formed for a purpose, and each member was added by God's design. Your group may desire more training and interaction with Muslims after completing the Bridges study. You may want to continue meeting to pray for Muslims or to organize group outreach events. We invite you to form an Oasis Team. For more information contact us at oasis@crescentproject.org.

Again, thank you for your diligence in leading a small group through Bridges. Be sure to register your group online and to access all of the bonus features just for you. And be sure to let us know the outcome of your study. We are here to serve you as your group shares the Hope with Muslims.

Reaching Muslims for Christ,

Fouad Masri

Fouad Masri
Executive Producer, Bridges
President, Crescent Project
www.fouadmasri.com

GETTING STARTED

REGISTERING GROUP MEMBERS ONLINE

Before you begin the session, have each group member provide his information on the roster available online. After the session register your group members online and remind them they can access the bonus features and additional information at www.bridgesstudy.com.

The First Two Sessions
The first two introductory sessions may contain information some students already know, like the Five Pillars of Islam and the life of Muhammad. For other students the information may be completely new. Whatever the case, make the students feel comfortable sharing and asking questions, especially if concepts seem confusing or sensitive. Admit that you may not have all of the answers, but you will do your best to answer difficult questions by the next class session.

SESSION 1: ISLAM RISING (pp. 7–18)

PRAYER (5 MIN.)

Open session 1 with prayer. When you pray, ask God to:

- Open the students' minds and hearts to Muslim people near them and around the world.
- Use the background information about Islam to help them understand Muslims.
- Place Muslims in their lives so that they will be able to share the love of Christ with them.

WARM-UP (5 MIN.)

This exercise will help the group get on the same page. If the students cannot think of anything, you may need to coach them along (for example: Do you know the founder of Islam? Do you know whom Muslims worship?) If they are unsure whether their previous knowledge of Islam is correct, they can record what they've read or heard through the media.

Allow three to five minutes to share their answers with the group.

VIDEO SESSION (30 MIN.)

Blanks:
1. A.D. 570
2. polytheistic
3. revelation
4. Mecca
5. idol worship
6. women
7. verse, verse
8. power
9. traditions

Leader's Notes

DISCUSSION (10 MIN.)

Question: John 3:16 says God sent Jesus because of His love for the world. From what you know about Islam, what can Jesus offer Muslims?

Suggested Responses
Jesus can offer Muslims:

✢ Assurance of salvation, to "not perish but have eternal life" (John 3:16). Muslims can never be sure whether they will go to heaven.

✢ God's love. It was demonstrated through sending Jesus Christ, the Word made flesh (see John 1:14; 3:16). Allah is known for 99 beautiful names, yet not one of them is agape love.

✢ Power to obey God and the capacity to genuinely love others (see John 15:5).

Ask the students to support their answers with Bible verses.

ACTION ASSIGNMENT (5 MIN.)

Ask students to be honest and committed in completing these Action Assignments. Encourage them to work in groups if that is more comfortable. The Action Assignment is an important step not only to enhance the training but also to impact the world around you. Let your group know you're there to help if they have any trouble with the assignment. Go online to *www.bridgesstudy.com* and get more ideas for connecting with Muslims in your community.

Bridges: Christians Connecting with Muslims

SESSION 2: BELIEF AND RITUAL (pp. 19–32)

PRAYER (5 MIN.)

Open session 2 with prayer. Pray that:

✢ Your basic understanding of Muslims' beliefs will give each of you credibility in their eyes.

✢ You can learn about Islamic rituals while growing in thankfulness for Christ's finished work on the cross (see Colossians 2:13-14).

✢ God will fill your hearts with compassion that results in action.

DISCUSSION (10 MIN.)

Give each student a chance to share the outcome of his/her Action Assignment. For large groups, you might ask one or two specific questions like "What is the name of your Muslim friend?" "What was new or surprising about the encounter?"

WARM-UP (5 MIN.)

The purpose of this exercise is to understand the difference between beliefs (what we think) and rituals or practices (what we do). Emphasize that good works in the life of a Christian are evidence of Christ's finished work (see Ephesians 2:8-10).

Note: Islamic practices or rituals are different from Christian practices in that they are not driven by a relationship with God. Instead, they are performed in submission to God.

Allow three to five minutes for group brainstorming.

Colossians 2:13-14
"He made you alive with Him and forgave us all our trespasses. He erased the certificate of debt, with its obligations, that was against us and opposed to us, and has taken it out of the way by nailing it to the cross."

VIDEO SESSION (30 MIN.)

Basic Islamic Beliefs
1. change his mind
2. name
3. character
4. Jinn
5. seal
6. Injeel
7. changed
8. good and evil

Pillars of Islam
9. Muslim
10. prayer ceremony
11. anytime or anywhere
12. washing
13. daylight
14. feasting
15. Final
16. Prayer requests
17. 2½ percent
18. 5 percent
19. once in his lifetime

DISCUSSION (5 MIN.)

Question: Why do you think memorizing Scripture from the Injeel, Tawrat, and Zabur might be helpful in sharing with Muslims?

Answers may include:
Muslims must believe these books, so they are familiar with the book but may not know its message. Muslims take the memorization of holy books very seriously. They may see your faith as legitimate when you are able to share verses from memory.

ACTION ASSIGNMENT (5 MIN.)

Encourage students to be diligent in completing the Action Assignment for this week. Maybe another topic other than holidays is more natural to discuss. The topics are merely suggestions to continue and deepen a friendship between a Christian and Muslim.

Note: The reference to Al-Makr on the video should be Qur'an 3:54 and Qur'an 8:30 instead of 8:3.

SESSION 3: ATTITUDES OF AN AMBASSADOR (pp. 33–44)

PRAYER (5 MIN.)

Open session 3 with prayer. Pray the students will:

✢ Conduct themselves with wisdom toward Muslims, making the most of every opportunity (see Colossians 4:5).

✢ Speak to Muslims in a way that is full of grace, as though seasoned with salt (see Colossians 4:6).

✢ Be ambassadors for Christ in all their interactions with Muslims (see 2 Corinthians 5:20).

WARM-UP (5 MIN.)

The purpose of this exercise is to anticipate topics or conversations with Muslims that are counterproductive. Examples could include politics, the Arab-Israeli conflict, terrorism, the treatment of women, etc. Suggest ways to navigate these topics that lead to Christ.

Example: In the case of the Arab-Israeli conflict, you could explain that the root cause of war and fighting is the sin of hatred. Jesus alone gives us power to love our enemy and forgive our neighbor.

Allow three to five minutes for group discussion.

Colossians 4:5-6
"Act wisely toward outsiders, making the most of the time. Your speech should always be gracious, seasoned with salt, so that you may know how you should answer each person."

Leader's Notes

VIDEO SESSION (30 MIN.)

Blanks:
1. represents
2. share
3. criticize
4. argue
5. similar
6. traditional
7. straightforward

DISCUSSION (5 MIN.)

Question: What approach do you think will be best to take with your friend?

Refer to the approach and the different types of Muslims in your notes from session 3. Suggested example: In the case of a highly educated, devout Muslim student, the best approach may be pursuing a friendship, with a focused effort not to argue. Extra study in Christian apologetics may be important.

ACTION ASSIGNMENT (5 MIN.)

Highlight the necessity of prayer. Remind students they can subscribe to Crescent Project's biweekly prayer e-mail, Call to Prayer, *www.crescentproject.org/calltoprayer*.

SESSION 4: BRIDGING THE GOSPEL (pp. 45–54)

PRAYER (5 MIN.)

Open session 4 with prayer. Pray for:

✢ Better understanding of the gospel of Jesus in light of what Muslims believe.

✢ Students to use this understanding to build bridges of truth to Muslims.

✢ Students to be the fragrance of Christ to Muslims by focusing on common ground.

WARM-UP (5 MIN.)

The Four Attitudes of an Ambassador are taken directly from session 3.

They are:
1. Loving
2. Friendly
3. Bridging
4. Biblical

If time allows, review the attitudes in more detail. Ask the group to give examples of when they demonstrated one or more of the four attitudes in an interaction with a Muslim.

Colossians 1:15
"He is the image of the invisible God, the firstborn over all creation."

DISCUSSION (5 MIN.)

In your opinion, what is the biggest difference between Islam and Christianity? Answers could include:

✢ **The character of God:** conditional love of Allah and unconditional love of God in the Bible

✢ **Grace and works:** earning God's favor and God's gift of grace

✢ **The person of Jesus Christ:** a prophet in Islam and the incarnate Word of God in Christianity

VIDEO SESSION (30 MIN.)

Blanks:

Basic Similarities
1. Holy One
2. Merciful
3. original sin
4. Jesus
5. Virgin Mary
6. Word of God
7. Intercessor

Basic Differences
8. physical relationship
9. win
10. changed
11. responsibility
12. stick

DISCUSSION (5 MIN.)

What fragrance does a follower of Christ bring?

✢ Followers of Christ spread the fragrance of knowing Christ (see 2 Corinthians 2:14).

✢ To God we are the aroma of Christ (see 2 Corinthians 2:15).

ACTION ASSIGNMENT (5 MIN.)

Keep in mind that some students may not have a Muslim friend yet. Encourage students to ask God to bring a Muslim into their lives. Next they must take the initiative to meet a Muslim. This could mean visiting a mosque, eating at an ethnic or Middle Eastern restaurant, or attending a cultural event. By session 4 it is important for each student to have at least one Muslim acquaintance to put their training into practice.

Bridges by Crescent Project

SESSION 5: TOOLS FOR REACHING MUSLIMS (pp. 55–68)
UNDERSTANDING THE NEW TESTAMENT'S CREDIBILITY

PRAYER (5 MIN.)

Open session 5 with prayer. Pray God will:

✟ Increase your confidence in the Bible's credibility.

✟ Give you natural opportunities to share the truth of God's Word with Muslims.

✟ Release His Word among Muslims in a way that does not return to Him empty but accomplishes the purposes for which He sent it (see Isaiah 55:11).

WARM-UP (5 MIN.)

Ask one or two group members to share their experiences meeting and befriending Muslims. What have been their greatest difficulties? What is the most helpful advice they have received so far? Another helpful question for discussion could be which Scriptures have had the greatest impact on students as they respond to Muslims.

VIDEO SESSION (30 MIN.)

Blanks:
1. meaning
2. judge
3. God forbid
4. humans
5. When
6. Where
7. before or after
8. living eyewitnesses
9. the same

Leader's Notes

DISCUSSION (5 MIN.)

Question: What does Fouad mean when he says, "Use the bridge as a thermometer"?

Suggested Answer
Using the bridge as a thermometer means testing the spiritual temperature of your Muslim friend. It may be that after sharing the theological reasoning (God is stronger than humans), your friend is open and willing to read the Injeel for himself. Or your friend may not be convinced until he or she understands the historical proof for the Bible's reliability. Try to gauge his or her interest by always starting with Mark 13:31 and the theological reasoning.

ACTION ASSIGNMENT (5 MIN.)

Encourage the students to relax and enjoy the friendship. Don't be so intent on sharing about the Injeel's credibility that you miss your friend's deeper need. There might be other spiritual questions you can answer.

Do you have a great testimony from your group? Share it with us at *bridges@crescentproject.org*.

Note: The full message of Is the Injeel Corrupted? *is included in your Companion Study Book, beginning on page 101, to review the concepts contained in this lesson. It is also available in book form for evangelistic purposes at www.crescentproject.org/bookstore.*

SESSION 6: TOOLS FOR REACHING MUSLIMS (pp. 69–78)

UNDERSTANDING JESUS' SACRIFICE

PRAYER (5 MIN.)

Open session 6 with prayer. Pray:

- Students will grasp the meaning of Abraham's willingness to sacrifice his son and what that means for Muslims today
- Muslims will be aware of their sin and need for a Savior
- For openings to share this truth with your Muslim friends

WARM-UP (5 MIN.)

Answers could include: God inspired the writing of the Injeel. The many versions are merely translations with the same message. On a theological level you could explain that God keeps His word and promised to keep the Injeel; He is stronger than men and will not allow mere humans to change His word.

On a logical level you could ask your friend where and when the Injeel was changed or who would commit such an act.

On a historical level you can explain the Zero-Corruption Bridge, spanning from Jesus death, burial, and resurrection to the modern day. If the Injeel was changed before Muhammad came, he should have instructed his followers to read the *unchanged* Injeel. He made no such distinction.

VIDEO SESSION (30 MIN.)

Blanks:
1. illogical
2. erase
3. judge
4. good works
5. sinner, sinner
6. 50/50
7. penalty
8. power
9. unique
10. redeemed
11. testify

DISCUSSION (10 MIN.)

Participants may refer to their Video Session notes if necessary. To begin the discussion, one member of the group might ask the other "Why did Jesus have to die?" or "Why should Jesus die for my sin? Each one must make up for his own sins." Then answer the questions by sharing the biblical verse first and then explaining the character of God and the need for a sacrifice. Remember to end with the Point of Decision.

Bridges: Christians Connecting with Muslims

ACTION ASSIGNMENT (5 MIN.)

Encourage the students to meet with their Muslim friend in an environment that lends itself to discussion and sharing. This will not be possible for some. If not, pray for the opportunity within the next few weeks.

Note: The full message of Adha in the Injeel *is included in your Companion Study Book, starting on page 133, to help you review the concepts contained in this lesson. These small booklets are available for evangelistic purposes in parallel Arabic/English at www.crescentproject.org/bookstore.*

Is the Injeel Corrupted?
My Search for Truth About the New Testament

FOUAD MASRI

Available as an eBook at www.fouadmasri.com

Dear Reader,

Praise God! Al Hamdulilah!

God gave me the strength to write this book, and I entrust to you my research on the Holy Injeel, the book given to Isa Al-Masih (Jesus the Christ), the son of Mary. God sent Al-Injeel to enlighten us to His will and commands so that we can live a life of faith. A life of faith in God (subhanahu wa ta'ala) is the greatest life someone could live. Faith is the fuel for meaning and success here on earth. For this reason I offer this book to our Ummah. May it be a blessing to our needy world.

Abd Allah (the servant of God),

Fouad Masri

CHAPTER 1

INTRODUCTION

"The Injeel is corrupted." You've heard it. Maybe you have even said it.

When I was growing up in the Middle East, it was common for my professors and fellow classmates to dismiss the Injeel. They said Christians have changed it, and over the years it has lost its real meaning.

In high school my friend Kamal told me I shouldn't read the Injeel since it was unreliable and had been changed by Christians.

"Have you read the Injeel?" I asked Kamal.

"No."

"Then how do you know it's corrupted?" I reasoned. "You haven't read it!"

"My grandfather and my uncle said so," he replied.

This ... led me to investigate why the Injeel was disregarded, concealed, and treated as taboo by my teachers and peers.

I probed further, only to find that his relatives who claimed the Injeel was corrupted had never read the book either.

This exchange and others led me to investigate why the Injeel was disregarded, concealed, and treated as taboo by my teachers and peers.

To my surprise I found the Injeel is required for Muslims to read and believe in. It is also required for Christians to share. While my friends were treating the Injeel like bad news, I found that Christians consider the Injeel good news.

THE MESSAGE OF GOD

Injeel is the Arabic word used for the Book of Prophet Jesus. *Evangelion,* the book's original Greek title, means *good news*. In Arabic the book was titled *Injeel,* and Arab Christians in pre-Islamic times used this word to refer to the New Testament, or the new covenant given by Christ.

The Injeel is the message of God for those who follow Jesus the Christ. The Injeel regulates every aspect of a Christian's life and beliefs.

Imams commonly teach that the Injeel is one of the four holy books Muslims are required to believe in, follow, and obey. If that is true, why is the Injeel not available in religious bookstores in many Muslim countries? If Muslims are to believe in the Injeel, why do some Islamic governments forbid their citizens to read it?

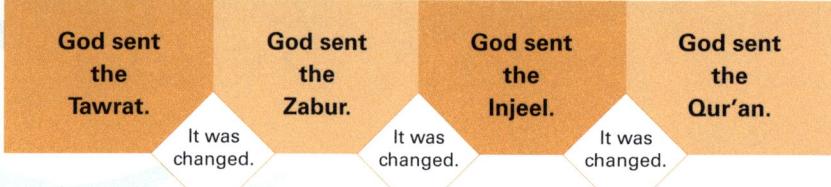

Is the Injeel really corrupted, as Kamal's uncle said it was? I wondered.

Muslims are obligated to honor Al-Qur'an Al-Karim and all of the holy books that God sent to humans: Al-Tawrat (the Book of Moses), Az-Zabur (the Book of David), and Al-Injeel (the Book of Jesus).

One man told me, "Muslims must honor these four books, but we follow only the Holy Qur'an" (Al-Qur'an Al-Karim). Therefore, the Injeel is not available in Muslim countries because many political and religious leaders believe the Injeel is corrupted. They follow the doctrine of tahrif, an idea that says Jews and Christians corrupted the original texts of the Tawrat and Injeel.

The common explanation is:

1. Al-Tawrat (the Book of Moses) was corrupted, so God sent Az-Zabur (the Psalms of David).
2. When Az-Zabur was corrupted, God sent Al-Injeel.
3. Finally, when Al-Injeel was corrupted, God sent Al-Qur'an Karim.
4. The Qur'an is incorruptible, for it is the word of God.

This illogical discourse stirred me to find out what it is about the Injeel that we are forbidden to know. Is the Injeel really corrupted? Did Christians change the Injeel?

I decided to study the Injeel and uncover its corruption for myself. I reasoned, *Why depend on the traditions of my community without investigating the facts? Most have never read the Injeel, yet they make judgments about its value. After all, many claimed the earth was flat until they studied the facts and found the earth is shaped as a sphere. Things are not always as they appear.*

The following is a summary of my research, which focused on answering a crucial question for those who submit to God: Is the Injeel corrupted?

CHAPTER 2
THE QUR'ANIC WITNESS
WHAT DOES THE QUR'AN SAY ABOUT THE INJEEL?

To begin, I wanted to learn what the Qur'an says about this good news, or Injeel. In the Qur'an (Al-Qur'an Al- Karim) the Injeel is also referred to as the Book of Jesus.

Al-Injeel Is Sent from God
"Allah! there is no god but He the Living the Self-Subsisting Eternal. It is He Who sent down to thee (step by step), in truth, the Book confirming what went before it; and He sent down the Law (Of Moses) and the Gospel (of Jesus) before this as a guide to mankind and He sent down the Criterion (of judgment between right and wrong)" (Qur'an 3:2-4).

Muslims Must Read and Believe in the Injeel
"Say ye: 'We believe in Allah and the revelation given to us and to Abraham, Isma'il, Isaac, Jacob, and the Tribes and that given to Moses and Jesus and that given to (all) Prophets from their Lord we make no difference between one and another of them and we bow to Allah (in Islam)' " (Qur'an 2:136).

"Then in their wake We followed them up with (others of) Our apostles: We sent after them Jesus the son of Mary and bestowed on him the Gospel; and We ordained in the hearts of those who followed him Compassion and Mercy" (Qur'an 57:27).

Christians Are Friends to Muslims
"*Nearest among them in love to the believers wilt thou find those who say: "We are Christians": because amongst these are men devoted to learning and men who have renounced the world, and they are not arrogant*" (Qur'an 5:82).

Christians Must Judge All Revelation by the Injeel
"*Let the people of the Gospel Judge by what Allah hath revealed therein*" (Qur'an 5:47).

"*Say: 'O People of the Book! Ye have no ground to stand upon unless ye stand fast by the Law, the Gospel, and all the revelation that has come to you from your Lord' *" (Qur'an 5:68).

God Keeps His Word
"*Allah hath power over all things*" (Qur'an 2:148).

To my surprise I learned that many imams are teaching what is contrary to the previous Qur'anic verses. They say Al-Tawrat was corrupted, so God sent Az-Zabur. When Az-Zabur was corrupted, God sent Al-Injeel. Finally, the Injeel was corrupted so God sent the Qur'an. The Qur'an is incorruptible, for it is the word of God.

However, the Qur'an, the holy book of Islam, never makes such a claim.

> **To my surprise I learned that many imams are teaching what is contrary to the Qur'an.**

CHAPTER 3

LET GOD BE TRUE
WHAT DOES THE INJEEL SAY ABOUT ITSELF?

The Qur'an seemed to point toward the credibility of the Injeel, but it seemed necessary to investigate the claims of the Injeel about itself. Listen to God's admonition and warning to Jews, Christians, and all humankind from the Injeel:

God Inspired All Scripture
"All Scripture is inspired by God and is profitable for teaching, for rebuking, for correcting, for training in righteousness, so that the man of God may be complete, equipped for every good work" (2 Timothy 3:16-17).

"No prophecy of Scripture comes from one's own interpretation, because no prophecy ever came by the will of man; instead, men spoke from God as they were moved by the Holy Spirit" (2 Peter 1:20-21).

God's Words Stand Firm and Will Be Fulfilled
"Don't assume that I came to destroy the Law or the Prophets. I did not come to destroy but to fulfill. For I assure you: Until heaven and earth pass away, not the smallest letter or one stroke of a letter will pass from the law until all things are accomplished" (Matthew 5:17-18).

"Heaven and earth will pass away, but My words will never pass away" (Matthew 24:35).

The Word of God Endures and Brings Life
"You have been born again—not of perishable seed but of imperishable—through the living and enduring word of God" (1 Peter 1:23).

God Protects His Word

"I testify to everyone who hears the prophetic words of this book: If anyone adds to them, God will add to him the plagues that are written in this book. And if anyone takes away from the words of this prophetic book, God will take away his share of the tree of life and the holy city" (Revelation 22:18-19).

Not only does the Injeel insist that God protects His Word, but the Zabur and Tawrat make this claim as well.

From the Tawrat

" 'As for Me, this is My covenant with them,' says the LORD: 'My Spirit who is on you, and My words that I have put in your mouth, will not depart from your mouth, or from the mouth of your children, or from the mouth of your children's children, from now on and forever,' says the LORD" (Isaiah 59:21).

From the Zabur

"LORD, Your word is forever; it is firmly fixed in heaven" (Psalm 119:89).

"Long ago I learned from Your decrees that You have established them forever" (Psalm 119:152).

"The entirety of Your word is truth, and all Your righteous judgments endure forever" (Psalm 119:160).

These verses stirred me. Christians would not dare alter or allow any change in their Holy Book, the Bible. Their respect for God and esteem for His commands are too great.

In fact, Christians would rather die than disobey and alter the Word of God.

After the resurrection of Jesus, His followers went from place to place proclaiming Christ as the Redeemer of the human race. Jewish leadership refused their words, and Roman and pagan emperors ridiculed what Jesus' followers said.

For Christianity's first three hundred years its followers were massacred, attacked, and tortured because of their faith, yet they refused to relent. As peaceful and pious people, they were unjustly abused for believing in Christ as the Savior of the universe. In many cases these martyrs of the Christian faith paved the way for the conversion of their persecutors.

The first Christians believed God's Word was true; they believed the previous verses show God as the powerful Creator of the universe who promised to keep and protect the Injeel.

CHAPTER 4

NO ONE IS STRONGER THAN GOD ALMIGHTY
A THEOLOGICAL INVESTIGATION

As a mu'min (believer in God), I could not reconcile how God's Word could be changed by mere humans. *If God revealed the Injeel*, I reasoned, *wasn't it His responsibility to keep it from corruption?* We know God is the Creator of the universe: the sun, stars, and moon—everything we see. He created humans, their minds, and their intellects. God sees the hearts and knows the inner thoughts of sheikhs and citizens, businessmen and shepherds, scientists and artists. His knowledge spans time zones and time periods. He knows the past, present, and future. God knows everything!

ARE HUMANS STRONGER THAN GOD?

If God's Word was revealed to humans, and humans corrupted God's Word, doesn't that make humans stronger than God? Impossible!

Once I assume it is possible for God's Word and message to be corrupted, then *mere humans* like me become the measure of all things and not God Almighty (subhanahu wa ta'ala).

God sent the Injeel to enlighten people to the truth, and Jesus said the truth would set us free. Certainly humans are not stronger than the God who created them! No, they cannot corrupt the Injeel since it is God's Word.

WHAT PROPHET JESUS BELIEVED ABOUT GOD'S WORD

Jesus the Christ is the beloved prophet of God Jesus the Christ is the beloved Prophet of God (Habib Allah). He was chosen before birth (Mustafa Allah) to become the Redeemer (Al-Fadi) of the universe.

In the Injeel Prophet Jesus makes a promise in Bisharat Marcus, chapter 13, Aya 31: "Heaven and earth will pass away, but My words will never pass away."

The Injeel also says in 2 Timothy 3:16, "All Scripture is inspired by God." He authored it, and it belongs to Him.

The Injeel is clear about its origin: "First of all, you should know this: No prophecy of Scripture comes from one's own interpretation, because no prophecy ever came by the will of man; instead, men spoke from God as they were moved by the Holy Spirit" (2 Peter 1:20-21).

FAITH IN GOD, DOUBT IN MAN

My faith in a mighty God made me doubt those religious teachers who claimed the Injeel was corrupted. Astagh'furallah! May God forbid that His Word could ever be tarnished by mere men.

Every time they accused the Injeel of being corrupted, they were blaspheming God. God sent the Injeel and has power over all things; He will preserve the Injeel as a testimony to all humans.

Astagh'furallah! May God forbid that His Word could ever be tarnished by mere men.

God is fair; He has protected His Word so that His verdict will be just when He judges each human by his or her response to the message of the Injeel.

No one can tamper with it. God has promised to keep it. And no one is stronger than God Almighty.

CHAPTER 5
ILLUSION VERSUS REALITY
A LOGICAL INVESTIGATION

Truth clearly stands out against error! God has given us the ability to seek truth, using not only our respect for God and His promises as a basis for belief but also logic and reasoning.

Humans are unique from all other creation in the way we gather information, process it, make conclusions about it, and finally transmit it to others. Our reasoning abilities are not threats to the truth; instead, they confirm it. If God created within me a mind that could reason, God would use this logic to support His own word and claims.

With this in mind, I set out to examine the corruption of the Injeel from a logical standpoint. Maybe God was not as powerful as I thought (Astagh'furallah).

The following pivotal questions and my deductive answers are the results of my search. In advance forgive my ignorance in doubting the power of God to keep His Word, the Injeel.

If the Injeel contained enlightenment about the existence of God and God's beautiful plan for the world, what would motivate someone to change that revelation?

SEVEN PIVOTAL QUESTIONS

1. Who changed the Injeel?
For the Injeel to be changed, there needs to be a person or persons in history responsible for plotting and carrying out this scheme.

Who is the person who centered his or her efforts on changing a message sent from God? What evil person would corrupt the Injeel, betraying God and Christians?

Was the corruption performed by a Christian who believed in God's justice and Christ as the Redeemer? Or could a pagan or Jewish zealot have done this deed?

If such an infidel existed, history must reveal the person who deleted some information or added to the text of the Injeel in the years following the life of Christ.

2. Why was the Injeel changed?
Why would such a person corrupt the Injeel? If the Injeel contained enlightenment about the existence of God and God's beautiful plan for the world, what would motivate someone to change that revelation?

If the Injeel was changed, why would God allow early Christians to live in ignorance of God's will for nearly six hundred years (the time between the Injeel's supposed corruption and the coming of the prophet of Islam)? People are in a continual quest to know God's will. Why destroy that sought-after treasure for many generations?

3. Where was the Injeel changed?
In what city or at what location was the Injeel corrupted? Did the discrepancy take place in a religious center or a political center? Which governments considered the Injeel a threat to them?

Rome, Byzantium, Alexandria, and Jerusalem—all of these were powerful epicenters of religious thought. But would any be more powerful than God Almighty? Can we find the original Injeel in that location and compare it to the present Injeel?

4. When was the Injeel changed?
At what point in history was the Injeel corrupted? According to Christian tradition, Jesus' death and resurrection occurred when Christ was in his 30s, making the event no earlier than A.D. 29 and no later than A.D. 33.

As we've already discussed, for three centuries after the life of Christ, Christians were persecuted and harshly oppressed. This leads us to a key question.

5. Did the Injeel's corruption take place before the coming of Prophet Muhammad or after?
Since the Prophet Muhammad commanded all Muslims to read the Injeel, it must have been corrupted after his death. He wouldn't have instructed us to believe and read a corrupted book, would he?

On the other hand, if the Injeel was corrupted before his time—or during his life—he surely would have mentioned it. If the Injeel has been corrupted since then, we need to go back in history and discover when.

6. Which parts were changed?
Many imams claimed corruption has found its way into the Injeel, but few would tell me which specific parts were affected.

Was the corruption thorough in that it affected the entire revelation of the Injeel? If so, is there any benefit to reading the message of the Injeel? If all of it is corrupted, why does the Qur'an require believing in it and reading it?

Perhaps only portions of the Injeel were changed. If only parts are corrupted, how can I discern truth from error? Was God able to protect some parts and not others?

7. Where is the original text?
This was a key question for me. All monotheistic religions affirm the coming of Jesus of Nazareth. So where is the true Injeel? As one devoted to God, I am required to study and respect the Injeel in obedience to God's commands. But how can I obey God by reading the Injeel if the original Injeel is lost? Would God allow such a mishap?

Because God sent Jesus and the Injeel to enlighten people for all generations, I must read the original text to fulfill my religious obligation.

THE FINAL REVELATION
One argument I heard was particularly intriguing. Some Muslim scholars pointed to the fact that since Islam came last chronologically, it had corrected the Injeel's errors and wrong ideas about God.

The Qur'anic verse most popularly used to support this idea was Qur'an 16:101-102:

"When We put a revelation in place of (another) revelation—and Allah knoweth best what He revealeth—they say: Lo! Thou art but inventing. Most of them know not.

"Say: The holy Spirit hath delivered it from thy Lord with truth, that it may confirm (the faith of) those who believe, and as guidance and good tidings for those who have surrendered (to Allah)."

Although the message of the Qur'an came last chronologically, its theological message is from the days of Prophet Abraham (Ibrahim), who called pagans to worship the one true God.

By the time the Qur'an was given to Muhammad, worshipers of one God had been guided for centuries by God's Word to Moses (Al-Tawrat), David (Az-Zabur), and Jesus (Al-Injeel).

Prophet Abraham (Ibrahim) was the first to submit himself to the one true God and turn away from his family's idolatrous past. He led his family from a pagan land to the place God led him.

The messages given to Moses (Musa), David (Daud), and Jesus (Isa) were primarily intended for a different audience altogether—the worshipers of one God. Therefore, God's revelation in the Tawrat, Zabur, and Injeel builds on the message of monotheism, carrying with it more advanced theological concepts, a greater understanding of God, and practical guidelines for living.

The culmination of God's revelation came through Prophet Jesus (Isa bin Maryam), the Word of God incarnate. His message was for all people, regardless of nationality, race, or language.

"Go, therefore, and make disciples of all nations, baptizing them in the name of the Father and of the Son and of the Holy Spirit, teaching them to observe everything I have commanded you. And remember, I am with you always, to the end of the age" (Matthew 28:19-20).

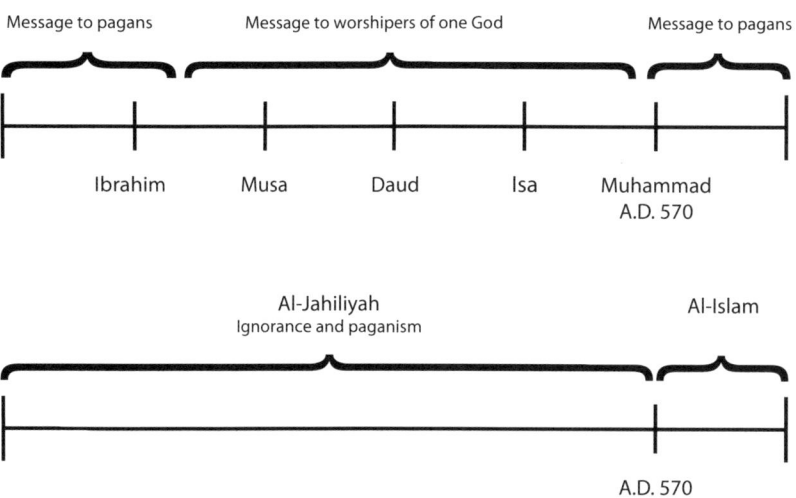

"I tell you that many will come from east and west, and recline at the table with Abraham, Isaac, and Jacob in the kingdom of heaven" (Matthew 8:11).

"There is no Jew or Greek, slave or free, male or female; for you are all one in Christ Jesus" (Galatians 3:28).

Is the Injeel Corrupted?

The Qur'an never presumes to replace the earlier messages from God.

The Qur'an, on the other hand, came to Arabs who were worshiping many gods and denied monotheism. This was Al-Jahiliyah, or the time of ignorance. It came as a wake-up call to the people of the Arabian Peninsula. Thus, the Qur'an's assertion that the message was in Arabic, to be understood by Arab tribes:

"We have made it a Qur'an in Arabic, that ye may be able to understand" (Az-Zukhruf 43:3).

In addition, the Qur'an repeatedly highlights that its message confirms what came before; it never presumes to replace the earlier messages.

"To thee We sent the Scripture in truth, confirming the scripture that came before it, and guarding it in safety: so judge between them by what Allah hath revealed" (Al-Ma'idah 5:48).

CHANGING THE WORDS OF GOD

Some Muslims cite the following verses in the Qur'an as evidence that Christians have changed the words of God.

"Those unto whom We gave the Scripture recognize (this revelation) as they recognize their sons. But lo! a party of them knowingly conceal the truth" (Al-Baqara 2:146).

"O followers of earlier revelation! Why do you cloak the truth with falsehood and conceal the truth of which you are [so well] aware?" (Al-Imran 3:71).

"Those who conceal the clear (Signs) We have sent down, and the Guidance, after We have made it clear for the people in the Book, 'on them shall be Allah's curse, and the curse of those entitled to curse'" (Al-Baqara 2:159).

The previous verses do not refer to people who changed the words of God but those who concealed it. God is stronger than any human, and while humans may try to conceal God's Word, His truth still clearly stands out from error.

FEAR OF TRUTH

In my search for answers to these questions, I was shocked by the ignorance of the religious leadership in my community. They seemed afraid of the questions; these ideas were not allowed to be discussed. I was accused of venturing where I should not go. *Why not read the Injeel?* I asked myself.

Some leaders tried to prove the corruption with dates, events, and places, but when I further investigated their claims, the only thing that became clear was their ignorance about the life of Prophet Jesus, the Injeel, and the Christian religion.

Friends of mine were hostile to my quest for truth. I was even harassed and questioned about my interest in reading and studying the New Testament.

Why the hostility? I was only looking for the Injeel so that I could become a good believer in God. Their logic was worse than their character. They were bloodthirsty instead of God-thirsty.

At this point my investigation led me to look at the historical evidence for the credibility of the Injeel and why Christians follow it.

CHAPTER 6

THE MANUSCRIPTS SPEAK
A HISTORICAL INVESTIGATION

My search for answers led me to an extensive examination of the historical context and manuscripts of the Injeel.

I discovered that the Injeel is highly revered among Christians. They have taken great care to protect it from corruption. The history of the Injeel can be divided into three historical time periods:
A. Eyewitness stage
B. Persecution stage
C. Translation stage

A. EYEWITNESS STAGE (A.D. 0–100)

Prophet Jesus (pbuh) was born to the virgin Mary as a miracle from God. His birth was foretold by prophets like Isaiah.

Virgin Birth Foretold
"The Lord Himself will give you a sign: The virgin will conceive, have a son, and name him Immanuel" (Isaiah 7:14).

City Foretold
"Bethlehem Ephrathah, you are small among the clans of Judah; One will come from you to be ruler over Israel for Me. His origin is from antiquity, from eternity" (Micah 5:2).

In the previous verses you can see that the coming of Prophet Isa (Jesus, the son of Mary) was prophesied hundreds of years in advance. The Tawrat was clear that the Messiah would come to lead people to the truth of God's law.

Jesus, the son of Mary, was the promised Messiah of the Jews.

"He first found his own brother Simon and told him, 'We have found the Messiah!' (which means 'Anointed One')" (John 1:41).

This same Jesus was sinless from birth and a leader of many believers. He raised the dead and healed the sick. His teachings and words were recorded in the book Al-Injeel.

Al-Injeel is Arabic for the Greek word *Evangelion*. Jesus and His followers spoke Koine Greek, the trade language under the Roman Empire. Scholars also agree that Jesus understood and spoke at least three languages: Koine Greek, Aramaic, and Hebrew.

Manuscripts
At present no one has found the original copies of any religious texts. We do not have the original, physical copy of Al-Qur'an Al-Karim, nor do we have Uthman's copy.

We also do not have the original, physical copy of the Tawrat, Zabur, or Injeel today. We have manuscripts that were hand copied and passed from one generation to another.

The scribes were serious about copying the Injeel because it was God's Word to enlighten humans. The Injeel warned them against tampering with the revelation of God in any way:

"I testify to everyone who hears the prophetic words of this book: If anyone adds to them, God will add to him the plagues that are written in this book. And if anyone takes away from the words of this prophetic book, God will take away his share of the tree of life and the holy city, written in this book" (Revelation 22:18-19).

EYEWITNESSES TO EVENTS IN THE INJEEL

While eyewitnesses to Jesus' birth, death, and resurrection were still living, any misrepresentation of Jesus' teachings or character would have been rejected. These people knew the truth.

"Many have undertaken to compile a narrative about the events that have been fulfilled among us, just as the original eyewitnesses and servants of the word handed them down to us. It also seemed good to me, since I have carefully investigated everything from the very first, to write to you in an orderly sequence" (Luke 1:1-3).

"We did not follow cleverly contrived myths when we made known to you the power and coming of our Lord Jesus Christ; instead, we were eyewitnesses of His majesty" (2 Peter 1:16).

We know these eyewitnesses firmly testified to what they had seen. What they wrote couldn't be disputed; everyone else had witnessed the same events and would correct them if they were wrong.

At the same time, if the followers of Christ incorrectly transcribed His words from the beginning, the Injeel and, subsequently, the Christian faith would never have existed.

To believe God sent the Injeel, we must first accept that God made sure it was recorded and copied correctly. Otherwise, people could not be judged by what was written in it. God's revelation must be perfect to ensure his righteous judgment.

In the eyewitness stage there was no opportunity for corrupting the Bible, because the eyewitnesses were alive. Those who were alive and knew the truth—whether believers or not—would protest any changes to the story.

For example, if I wrote a history book claiming John F. Kennedy was never assassinated or Martin Luther King Jr. never gave his famous "I have a dream" speech or that America's astronauts never walked on the moon, people would dismiss it as heresy; eyewitnesses to JFK's assassination, King's speech, and the U.S. moonwalk are still living. In 50 to 100 years people might consider buying my book. But as long as the eyewitnesses are alive, I cannot deny or re-create any major historical events.

The same is true for the major events in the Injeel. No one during the eyewitness stage could dispute a historical fact.

In addition to these eyewitnesses being alive and attesting to the truth of the Injeel's message, two other facts—martyrdom and the proof of the resurrection—also contribute to the Injeel's trustworthiness:

1. No one will die for a lie they made up.
Usually people lie for personal gain or to cover an embarrassing situation. Many followers of Prophet Jesus died claiming that Jesus is the Messiah who died and rose again.

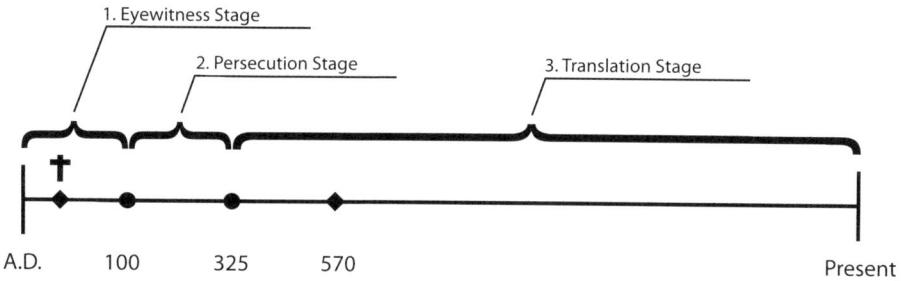

2. No conclusive evidence was available for Jesus' staying in the grave.
Eyewitnesses who were opposed to Christ could have brought the body of Jesus to Christians as proof that denies the resurrection. If they could have, they would have!

Such is the case with the Injeel in this stage. The eyewitness stage begins at the birth of Jesus and ends in the year A.D. 100. The last eyewitnesses to Jesus' life, death, and resurrection could not have survived after the year A.D. 100. The community of eyewitnesses—whether following Christ or not—would have died by A.D. 100.

After the last eyewitness died around A.D. 100, the first opportunity to change God's Word would arise. If an infidel wanted to corrupt God's Word, he now had his chance.

B. PERSECUTION STAGE (A.D. 100–325)

In this time period Christians everywhere were persecuted. Jewish leaders harassed and killed them. The Romans considered them atheists since they did not believe in a pantheon of gods. Considering Christians a great threat, Romans ordered them killed and burned along with their books.

In this age of persecution against Jesus' followers, it is highly unlikely that changes entered the Injeel. The four evidences proving the Injeel's integrity during this time period are:
1. Manuscripts
2. Lectionaries
3. Early translations
4. Church fathers

Let's take a deeper look at each piece of evidence.

1. Manuscripts

The books of the New Testament were copied by hand on manuscripts made of papyri. Papyrus is a plant that grows in Egypt. When Egyptians invented paper from papyri, different colors of ink were used to write in hieroglyphs.

A Brief History

The Phoenicians borrowed the Egyptian's invention and wrote using the alphabet, spreading the message to the known world from Byblos. The early Christians started copying the books of the Injeel as the manuscripts deteriorated and new churches were established. When the last surviving disciple, John, was exiled to and died on the island of Patmos, Christians copied the books of the Injeel with renewed passion, distributing them among the churches.

Most members of the Christian community couldn't afford a personal copy of the entire Injeel. Partial manuscripts—a few books of the New Testament, not the entire text—were therefore produced, distributed, and shared among Christian believers.

Another type of partial manuscript is the copies of the Injeel found in the ruins of Christian homes and churches. These are partial due to age or deterioration through time, not original copy.

Partial manuscripts dating from A.D. 100 to A.D. 325 include the whole books of the Injeel, accounts of the crucifixion and resurrection of Christ, and records of the uniqueness of Jesus and His atoning death.

2. Lectionaries
The existence of church lectionaries is one of the most important evidences of the New Testament's credibility, yet it is often the least studied, least known, and least used. Lectionaries contain the appointed readings (or "lections") for each day of the church year. As such, they were extremely important to individual churches.

Since many Christians did not own a personal copy of the Injeel, they depended on these service books for learning and growing in the knowledge of God's Word.

The number of known lectionaries has jumped to about 2,300 copies. In addition, almost 3,200 continuous-text manuscripts exist, bearing witness to the widespread and widely read nature of the Injeel during this time frame.

3. Early Translations
Complete manuscripts of the Injeel translated from Greek to other Mediterranean languages are important in verifying the New Testament's reliability. One such copy in Syriac is known as the Peshitto. Translations such as this can be reverse translated to check its reliability with the original Greek manuscripts.

4. Church Fathers

Leaders of the Christian community who were followers of Christ's disciples were known as church fathers.[1] You could call them second-generation disciples.

Following Christ under severe persecution, they led their communities to faith in Christ. While living in different areas around the Mediterranean Sea, they corresponded with one another through written letters and sermons. Their writings are still available today for study and comparison to the earliest complete manuscript (Codex Sinaiticus) in existence.

These letters and sermons have been uncovered around the Mediterranean Sea, with quotations and passages in total agreement with today's texts.

C. TRANSLATION STAGE (A.D. 325–PRESENT)

The Injeel was faithfully copied and distributed as Christianity spread throughout Europe and Asia. As the Injeel was reproduced into different languages, translators were meticulous in keeping each copy consistent with the manuscripts.

All versions or translations in other languages are copied from these early manuscripts:
1. Codex Sinaiticus
2. Codex Vaticanus
3. Codex Alexandrinus

---

1. A partial listing of church fathers:

Early Church
A.D. 301	Alexander, Bishop of Lycopolis
A.D. 260–311	Peter, Bishop of Alexandria

Apostolic Fathers
A.D. 30–100	Saint Clement
A.D. 130	Mathetes, "the Unknown Disciple"
A.D. 69–155	Polycarp
A.D. 30–107	Ignatius John Papias
A.D. 70–155	Justin Martyr
A.D. 110–165	Irenaeus

A careful look at Christian history from the death and resurrection of Christ to the present day reveals a thread of faithfulness to the preservation of God's revealed Word.

Versions

Some claim that the many different versions of the Injeel have corrupted its intended meaning. *Version* in English means *translation*. When famous Muslim debaters claim that a version of the Bible means another version of the story, they are only exposing their ignorance of the English language.

Some who claim to be an authority on the Christian Bible are ignorant of basic Hebrew and Greek, the primary languages of the Bible. Just as it is absurd

for a person untrained in Arabic to claim himself an authority on the Qur'an, it is just as important to learn the biblical languages (Hebrew and Koine Greek) to be an authority on the Bible.

History Is Speaking

What is history saying to us? A careful look at Christian history from the death and resurrection of Christ to the present day reveals a thread of faithfulness to the preservation of God's revealed Word.

From first-century eyewitness accounts (eyewitness stage) to quoted Scripture in letters sent among persecuted believers (persecution stage) to the early copies of God's Word available from as early as A.D. 325 (translation stage), the manuscripts are speaking to us. They are speaking the same consistent message of Jesus today that was lived and recorded nearly two thousand years ago.

"[Jesus] said, 'Anyone who has ears to hear should listen!'" (Mark 4:9).

> The book we hold in our hands today is the same story believed by the early followers of Jesus. They lived and died by that firm belief.

CHAPTER 7

WHAT DOES ALL THIS MEAN?

In this study I have attempted to understand my friends' and neighbors' unfounded claims that the Injeel is corrupted. What I found not only convinced me the Injeel has been preserved and kept by God but also challenged me to believe and stake my life on its message.

Historically, the overwhelming evidence available to us today not only speaks; it shouts! The evidence only verifies the truth and pure nature of the Injeel. The manuscripts and early textual proofs clearly point to the truth about the Injeel. The book we hold in our hands today is the same story believed by the early followers of Jesus. They lived and died by that firm belief.

Logically, we found that one must answer some pivotal questions before he accuses the Injeel of corruption, questions such as:
- When was the Injeel corrupted?
- Who would do such a thing?
- What motivation would someone have to change the Injeel?

Besides, it is unlikely that the closest adherents and followers of a religion—all twelve disciples—would die for their beliefs if they had been lying all along.

Many who claimed the Injeel was corrupted were simply misinformed about its origin and message. Their claims were not supported by any research or logical proof. Because of their ignorance they have led many away from the path of understanding. In an attempt to speak for God, they have failed to give Him the respect and admiration He deserves for protecting and keeping the Injeel!

Finally, in order to believe in a Creator with power over all things, a God who communicates with His creation and remains a just Judge based on what He has revealed, one must accept that God sent us His Word, Jesus. We must accept that the Injeel has been protected by God for the sake of humanity's enlightenment (lihuda al-alamiin).

God Almighty used this study to compel me to faith in God and the Redeemer, Jesus the Messiah. Today I invite you to enter the family of Jesus by making the following prayer. Christ can give you power to live in obedience to God.

Prayer is simply a conversation with God Almighty, done anywhere you are, at any time of day or night.

Almighty God, You are the merciful God. I repent of my sin and self-righteous attitude. I believe in You and Your Word, Jesus the Messiah. I commit to follow your teachings in the Injeel until my last breath.

Amen.

APPENDIX 1
TERMS

Allah—the Arabic name for God, meaning *the one God*.

Astagh'furallah—the Arabic word used by Christians and Muslims to entreat forgiveness in the event of blasphemous words or sinful behavior.

codex—a type of manuscript that consists of pages of papyri with writings on front and back. These are collected in a specific order and bound by leather or wood.

imam—the lay religious leader or professional cleric of a Muslim community or mosque; leads in Friday salat (noon congregational prayers).

Injeel—the Arabic name given to the Book of Jesus. It is mentioned in the Qur'an as the book revealed to Prophet Jesus and followed by Christians, the New Testament.

Isa—the Qur'anic and Arabic name for Jesus (English) or Yesua (Hebrew). In the Qur'an Jesus is called Kalimat Allah, "the Word of God," "the breath from God," and "a prophet of the Book." Muslims consider Jesus to be one of the five or six authentic prophets.

Isa al-Masih—Jesus the Messiah

manuscripts—earliest known writings of religious texts from which all subsequent translations are based.

Muhammad—praised; the chosen one, the prophet and founder of Islam, considered by Muslims to be khatem al-anbiya, the Seal (last) and greatest of the prophets. Born A.D. 570, died A.D. 632.

mu'min—believer; in contrast to an unbeliever, kafir.

Tawrat—the Qur'anic name given to the Torah of Moses.

ummah—community; a group bound by ancestry, religion, nation, race, occupation, or common cause.

Zabur—the Qur'anic name given to the Psalms of David.

APPENDIX 2
NICENE (OR NICAEAN) COUNCIL

The Nicene Council was an ecumenical or worldwide council that sought to unify the Christian church by addressing certain issues relating to the Christian faith. Although previous church councils had met throughout Christian history, the Council of Nicaea was important due to its sponsorship by the Emperor Constantine.

In A.D. 325 Constantine invited bishops and church leaders from the Mediterranean and beyond to the meeting held in Nicaea, Asia Minor, near what was then Constantinople.

Discussion centered on the religious texts read and taught in churches and their implications for the Christian faith. The leaders sought to answer this question: What, of these texts, is not the Word of God?

The criteria set resulted in what is known today as the New Covenant (to Arab Christians, the Injeel). Some texts that failed to meet the strict criteria were called Pseudo pigroipha (today Pseudepigrapha), or false writings.

Books categorized as Pseudepigrapha were written by individuals who were not contemporaries of Jesus or eyewitnesses to his life, death, and resurrection.

The Nicene Council developed criteria for what is not considered the Word of God. Many wrongfully accuse the Nicene Council for deciding what Scripture was the Word of God. Instead, the council simply affirmed what the church for centuries had considered inspired and developed criteria for determining errant texts.

APPENDIX 3
CARBON DATING OF MANUSCRIPTS

Radiocarbon dating is a radiometric dating method that uses the naturally occurring isotope carbon-14 to determine the age of carbonaceous materials. In addition to binding, handwriting, and paper type, it is one of the methods commonly used to date ancient manuscripts.

Through the use of radiocarbon dating and other factors such as handwriting, historians generally agree on the dates for the three earliest manuscripts of the New Testament.

They are:

Codex Vaticanus (A.D. 300)—has resided in the Vatican since the Middle Ages and remains there today.

Codex Sinaiticus (A.D. 350)—on permanent display in the British Library along with other early biblical manuscripts.

Codex Alexandrinus (A.D. 450)—transferred from the Christian Library in Alexandria to the British Library in the 17th century, where it still resides today.

APPENDIX 4
TRANSLATIONS OF THE BIBLE

The Injeel was originally written in Koine Greek, the language of the common people in the Roman Empire. Scholars have taken great care to translate the Bible's message into many languages so that people from all nations and backgrounds can read and understand it.

Some people might accuse translators of changing the meaning of the New Testament. This is far from the truth. Committees of dedicated scholars ensure that every translation reflects the original Greek texts. Christians consider the Bible a holy Book, handling it with respect and honoring the original manuscript in every translation.

In the final analysis those who doubt the credibility of individual translations should consider studying Koine Greek in order to read the New Testament in its earliest form. When I did that, I found the study of the New Testament Greek manuscripts to be fruitful and intellectually—as well as spiritually—satisfying. I trust you will find it the same.

APPENDIX 5
THE FIVE PILLARS OF CHRISTIANITY: WHAT EVERY CHRISTIAN BELIEVES

Did you know Christians across the face of the earth are unified by five core beliefs? We call these the Five Pillars of Christianity.

1. **One God—Christians believe in one God.**
   "Even if there are so-called gods, whether in heaven or on earth—as there are many 'gods' and many 'lords'—yet for us there is one God, the Father. All things are from Him, and we exist for Him" (1 Corinthians 8:5-6).

2. **One Savior—Christians are redeemed by one Savior.**
   "[Grace] has now been made evident through the appearing of our Savior Christ Jesus, who has abolished death and has brought life" (2 Timothy 1:10).

3. **One Spirit—Christians are filled and empowered by one Spirit.**
   "You will receive power when the Holy Spirit has come on you, and you will be My witnesses in Jerusalem, in all Judea and Samaria, and to the ends of the earth" (Acts 1:8).

4. **One message—Christians are unified by one message.**
   "Jesus went to Galilee, preaching the good news of God: 'The time is fulfilled, and the kingdom of God has come near. Repent and believe in the good news!' " (Mark 1:14-15).

5. **One family—Christians are part of one family.**
   "There is no Jew or Greek, slave or free, male or female; for you are all one in Christ Jesus." (Galatians 3:28).

Adha in the Injeel

FOUAD MASRI
Available as an eBook at www.fouadmasri.com

Muslims around the world annually celebrate the feast of Al-Adha. This feast takes place on the 10th of Dhul-Hijat, a month in the Muslim lunar calendar.

The root word for Adha is the Arabic word Dahiya, which means sacrifice. The Al-Adha feast is also known as the Feast of Sacrifice or the Great Feast, Id Al-Kabir. In the Turkic world the Adha feast is known as Qurbani.

At the Al-Adha feast many Muslims sacrifice a sheep or a ram to commemorate the holy event when God redeemed the son of Abraham. This incident is recorded in the Qur'an in Sura 37:99-111.

The Jewish religion also believes in this same holy event when God redeemed the son of Abraham with a ram. When Abraham was about to sacrifice his son, the angel of the Lord stopped him. Abraham looked and saw a ram caught in the thicket by its horns. He took the ram and sacrificed it as a burnt offering. The full record of this event is found in the Tawrat, the Book of Genesis 22:1-19.

Although the Jewish religion does not commemorate this specific event with a feast, the same idea and meaning are included in the Passover that was given to them by the prophet Moses. Jews celebrate the Passover to commemorate the night when God spared the Jewish firstborn from being slain in Egypt. The angel of death passed over the houses of those who put the blood of a slaughtered sheep at their doorposts, without harming their firstborn. The Passover is recorded in the Tawrat, the Book of Exodus 12:1-14.

Where is the Christian Adha?

Since Christians believe in both the Passover and the Adha events, why don't they celebrate them? Is there a Christian Passover too? To answer these questions, we need to look in the Injeel (the New Testament) and examine its teachings on the character of God and His plan for humankind.

1 THE INJEEL TEACHES THAT
GOD IS LOVE

God is the Creator of the universe and seeks fellowship with his creation. God's joy and pleasure is to communicate with humans, the highest of creation, bestowed with both a mind and a will.

The Injeel says:
"God is love, and the one who remains in love remains in God, and God remains in him" (1 John 4:16).

"I [Jesus] have come that they may have life and have it in abundance" (John 10:10).

Since God seeks fellowship with humans, why is our world so far from God? Why do people feel separated from God? It seems as if a great gulf separates us from enjoying God and His love.

2 THE INJEEL TEACHES THAT
GOD IS HOLY

God is holy and righteous, and humans are sinful. Everywhere we turn, we see the sinfulness of humans. Their actions are symptoms of the real disease of Sin. Sin is rebellion against God.

All humans have sinned. Sin is choosing our way instead of God's way. All humans fall short of perfectly obeying God's standard and law. Since the days of Adam, all people have chosen to go their own way rather than to obey God. This disobedience is what the Injeel calls sin.

We have all sinned against God Almighty and cannot remove our guilt. A righteous God is holy and cannot fellowship with sinful people.

> **Since God seeks fellowship with humans, why is our world so far from God? Why do people feel separated from God?**

The Injeel affirms that all have sinned against a holy God:

"There is no one righteous, not even one. There is no one who understands; there is no one who seeks God. All have turned away; all alike have become useless. There is no one who does what is good, not even one" (Romans 3:10-12).

"All have sinned and fall short of the glory of God" (Romans 3:23).

HOLY GOD SIN SINFUL HUMANS

Humans need God the way a lightbulb needs electricity. A lightbulb without electricity is dead, lifeless, and aimless.

3 THE INJEEL TEACHES THAT GOD IS JUST

The Injeel continues to explain that sin is what separates us from our loving and holy God. God's holiness condemns sin. The very righteous character of God cannot accept sin. Therefore, God and humans are separated by a great gulf, which is sin.

This separation from God results in spiritual death.

The Injeel says:
"The wages of sin is death" (Romans 6:23).

The wages of sin is death, yet no sinner can die to redeem someone else. This makes a great gulf between Holy God and sinful men and women.

Humans need God the way a lightbulb needs electricity. A lightbulb without electricity is dead, lifeless, and aimless. Sin has separated humans from God and made us spiritually dead, lifeless, and aimless.

God's justice compels Him to punish and destroy sin. We have sinned against God Almighty, and the penalty is death. God cannot forgive a sinful person until that sinful person's debt is paid. Mere good works, such as fasting or giving alms to the poor, cannot pay the debt by earning God's favor. Even the most noble acts fall short of God's perfect holiness and justice. Our best is not good enough to please a perfect God, which means every single person—even the best of us—has sinned and must be punished.

A criminal cannot redeem another criminal; simply put, all humans have sinned and have fallen short of God's law. God's holiness and justice do not allow forgiveness without payment of this huge debt. We have chosen our own way and have broken God's commandment, so we must pay the penalty. That penalty is separation from God.

4 THE INJEEL TEACHES THAT
GOD IS MERCIFUL

God's mercy sought to provide an answer to this problem. God wants to fellowship with us, his creation, but sin has created a gulf between him and us.

Only a righteous person can cross over the gulf to God. However, we have already established that everyone has sinned and has fallen short!

Everyone, that is, except Jesus Christ. The Injeel teaches that Jesus Christ is the only bridge between a holy God and sinful humans. **Why Jesus and not anyone else?**

Miraculous Birth

The Injeel teaches that Jesus Christ was not the son of a human father but was conceived by the power of the Holy Spirit in the womb of the virgin Mary. He was the only person to be born of a virgin. Jesus Christ's birth was not a result of the will of man but the will of God.

Jesus Christ is unique in His miraculous birth. No prophet or leader has been born from a virgin. All prophets claimed they were just humans, while Jesus Christ claimed He was the Word of God, Kalimat Allah. God's power is responsible for this miracle.

"The angel told her: 'Do not be afraid, Mary, for you have found favor with God. Now listen: You will conceive and give birth to a son, and you will call His name Jesus. He will be great and will be called the Son of the Most High, and the Lord God will give Him the throne of His father David. He will reign over the house of Jacob forever, and His kingdom will have no end.' Mary asked the angel, 'How can this be, since I have not been intimate with a man?' The angel replied to her: 'The Holy Spirit will come upon you, and the power of the Most High will overshadow you. Therefore, the holy One to be born will be called the Son of God. And consider your relative Elizabeth—even she has conceived a son in her old age, and this is the sixth month for her who was called childless. For nothing will be impossible with God' " (Luke 1:30-37).

Miraculous Life

Jesus Christ lived a life of purity and honesty. He was obedient to the laws of God throughout His life. Jesus Christ taught like no one else and miraculously healed every weakness and disease. He was sinless from birth and was considered the greatest teacher who ever lived.

"Jesus was going all over Galilee, teaching in their synagogues, preaching the good news of the kingdom, and healing every disease and sickness among the people. Then the news about Him spread throughout Syria. So they brought to Him all those who were afflicted, those suffering from various diseases and intense pains, the demon-possessed, the epileptics, and the paralytics. And He healed them. Large crowds followed Him from Galilee, Decapolis, Jerusalem, Judea, and beyond the Jordan" (Matthew 4:23-25).

Jesus Christ did not come to earth merely to be a good teacher or healer. He came to be the sacrifice of God.

Miraculous Death

Jesus Christ did not come to earth merely to be a good teacher or healer. He came to be the sacrifice of God. Because Jesus Christ is righteous, sinless from birth, His death alone can pay the penalty for sin. He came to redeem humanity from its fallen state. The Injeel clearly states that all have sinned against God and need salvation. Salvation means to be pardoned by God because someone paid the penalty we could not pay ourselves.

Jesus Christ, the only righteous one, willingly paid the debt we owe. Humans are dead in sin. Sin is the gulf that separates us from God. Jesus Christ was crucified and died as a righteous sacrifice for the human race. Just as Abraham sacrificed a ram instead of his son, Jesus' death on the cross was the sacrifice to pay the penalty of the sin of all humankind. The sheep died so that the son of Abraham could be set free. Likewise, Jesus died so that we can be set free. For as God redeemed the son of Abraham with a ram, likewise God redeemed the world through Jesus Christ.

As Muslims sacrifice a sheep at Al-Adha and the Israelites sacrificed a sheep during Passover in Egypt, God made Jesus Christ the perfect sacrifice for our sins.

Jesus became the true Adha. He was the Lamb of God to lift away the sins of the world. John the Baptist (known as the prophet Yahya) prophesied when he saw Jesus and said:

Our sin insults God's righteousness; only Jesus' sacrificial work can suffice.

"Here is the Lamb of God, who takes away the sin of the world!" (John 1:29).

Through Jesus Christ, God bridged the gulf that separated us from Him.

"Everything is from God, who reconciled us to Himself through Christ and gave us the ministry of reconciliation" (2 Corinthians 5:18).

The justice of God was satisfied, for the penalty of sin was paid. The mercy of God was satisfied, for humans have redemption.

Miraculous Resurrection

Jesus Christ paid the penalty for our sin so that we can have fellowship with God.

Jesus Christ is righteous and did not deserve death. He is the Word of God, Kalimat Allah. Jesus is the incarnate Word of God becoming the sacrifice for our salvation.

Christ rose from the dead on the third day according to prophecy. Christ's resurrection proved that His sacrifice was acceptable to God.

"I passed on to you as most important what I also received: that Christ died for our sins according to the Scriptures, that He was buried, that He was raised on the third day according to the Scriptures, and that He appeared to Cephas, then to the Twelve. Then He appeared to over 500 brothers at one time; most of them are still alive, but some have fallen asleep" (1 Corinthians 15:3-6).

Christians around the world celebrate the Adha and the Passover in one glorious celebration of the crucifixion and resurrection of Jesus Christ (known in English as Easter and in Arabic as Id Al-Qiama). This is the Adha and Passover come true!

These holy events were object lessons God used so that we could understand true redemption. The Bible says that the blood of calves and sheep will not wash away sins and that all our good works are like filthy rags compared to God's righteousness. No one can possibly pay the huge debt that is owed to God.

The good news is that God sent Jesus Christ to be the sacrificial Lamb of God who takes the sins of the world.

Jesus Christ Is Our True Adha!
Let's say a friend of mine asks me to watch his house while he travels and I accidentally destroy the furniture. However, before his return, I wash his car. Would that cover the cost of replacing the furniture? No! If I ask my friend to have mercy and forgive me for destroying his furniture since I washed the car, is it acceptable? No!

Even if he forgave me, my friend still has to pay for new furniture. Likewise, our good works are not righteous enough compared to God's righteousness. Our good works will never erase sin, for we are expected to do good and obey God's commandments.

Our sin insults God's righteousness; only Jesus' sacrificial work can suffice. Only the Christian Adha covers the debt of our sin and bridges the gap.

The Christian Adha is available to everyone, for Christ came to save all people, of all nations and races. Through Christ we can cross over to fellowship with God and experience His love and redemption.

5 THE INJEEL TEACHES THAT
GOD IS FORGIVING

It is not enough to know that God has found an Adha for sin. Each one of us needs to receive this sacrifice in a personal and humble decision.

We experience God's forgiveness in the following way. We must repent of our sin and receive Jesus Christ as Lord and Savior in order to experience God's love and forgiveness.

Repentance is turning to God from our own sinful ways and receiving God's offer of forgiveness, made possible by Christ's work on the cross (the Christian Adha).

The Injeel says:

"If we confess our sins, He is faithful and righteous to forgive us our sins and to cleanse us from all unrighteousness" (1 John 1:9).

- God forgives our sins if we confess them because Christ paid the debt.
- The perfect justice of God demanded punishment.
- The mercy of God was shown in the Christian Adha.
- Forgiveness can be granted because the justice of God was satisfied.
- Forgiveness can be enjoyed by repentant sinners because Christ paid the debt.

Sin dwells within the heart of every human being. The human race is in need of a "heart transplant," a new life that will change a sinner to a saint. The Injeel says:

"The wages of sin is death, but the gift of God is eternal life in Christ Jesus our Lord" (Romans 6:23).

The Christian Adha released us from spiritual death and offered us eternal life. God's gift of eternal life is in accepting Christ's sacrifice for our sin. We receive Christ's sacrifice by faith (trust).

Christ's sacrifice is free yet priceless. We must receive it by faith. We can do nothing to earn it ourselves.

"You are saved by grace through faith, and this is not from yourselves; it is God's gift—not from works, so that no one can boast" (Ephesians 2:8-9).

The gift of God cannot be enjoyed unless it is received. We receive Christ and His sacrificial work by a personal commitment.

"To all who did receive Him, He gave them the right to be children of God, to those who believe in His name, who were born, not of blood, or of the will of the flesh, or of the will of man, but of God" (John 1:12-13).

Christ is seeking to enter our lives, cleanse us from sin, and mend our broken relationship with God. Christ wants to be our Lord and Savior. Jesus says in the Injeel:

"Listen! I stand at the door and knock. If anyone hears My voice and opens the door, I will come in" (Revelation 3:20).

Prayer is talking to God. We can pray to God wherever we are and whenever we want. To receive Christ's sacrifice (the Christian Adha), we are to pray to God and know by faith (by trusting God) that we have salvation.

Your prayer to God can be something like this:

Dear Lord, thank You for Your love for me. I ask Your forgiveness because of Christ's atoning death. I open the door of my life and receive Jesus Christ as my Lord and Savior. Make me a new person. Thank You for giving me eternal life. In Jesus' name. Amen.

Pray this prayer and ask Christ to enter your life, forgive your sins, and restore your fellowship with God. If you sincerely asked Christ to enter your life, be assured that He did.

It is important to know that God's promises are true.

It is important to know that God's promises are true. In Revelation 3:20 Christ says, "I stand at the door and knock, if anyone hears my voice and opens the door, I will come in." If you opened the door of your life and asked Christ to enter as Savior and Lord, He will not deceive you. Christ is faithful.

The Injeel teaches that Jesus Christ is faithful to His promises:

"If you remain in Me and My words remain in you, ask whatever you want and it will be done for you" (John 15:7).

"I will never leave you or forsake you" (Hebrews 13:5).

"Jesus Christ is the same yesterday, today, and forever" (Hebrews 13:8).

"I know the One I have believed in and am persuaded that He is able to guard what has been entrusted to me until that day" (2 Timothy 1:12).

"I am sure of this, that He who started a good work in you will carry it on to completion until the day of Christ Jesus" (Philippians 1:6).